# An Introduction to
# Cost and Production Functions

## ALSO BY DAVID F. HEATHFIELD

*The Econometric Study of the UK* (editor)

*Production Functions*

*Topics in Applied Macroeconomics* (editor)

*The Economics of Co-determination* (editor)

*Perspectives on Inflation: Models and Policy* (editor)

# AN INTRODUCTION TO COST AND PRODUCTION FUNCTIONS

David F. Heathfield
and
Sören Wibe

MACMILLAN
EDUCATION

First published 1987

Published by
MACMILLAN EDUCATION LTD
Houndmills, Basingstoke, Hampshire RG21 2XS
and London
Companies and representatives
throughout the world

Printed in Hong Kong

British Library Cataloguing in Publication Data
Heathfield, David F.
An introduction to cost and production functions.
1. Production functions (Economic theory)
I. Title   II. Wibe, Sören
338'.001     HB241
ISBN 0–333–36580–1 (hardcover)
ISBN 0–333–41607–4 (paperback)

# Contents

## 5 The CES Function   92

## 6 The Translog Function   105

## 7 Technological Progress   118

**8**  **From Firms to Industry: the Johansen Production Model   134**

**9**  **Empirical Work on Production Functions   153**

# Authors' Preface

There can be little doubt that production functions, and their associated cost functions, form an integral part of an enormous range of economic theory. In microeconomics, production functions underlie the supply side of markets, generate production possibility frontiers, offer an explanation of income distribution and yield factor demand functions. Production functions are also central to the theory of economic growth and to investigations into the rate of technological progress. In international trade, production functions are used to provide a rationale for product and factor movements across national boundaries. In macroeconomics, production functions lie behind aggregate supply functions, aggregate labour demand functions and form the link between output and the consequent employment. Even the demand side can make use of production functions. The functional forms used for utility functions are often 'borrowed' from production theory. Indeed the production model has been transferred wholesale to model 'demand'.

It is clear from this somewhat impressive list that a knowledge of production functions is a useful if not essential part of being an economist.

The kind of production function most widely used is the so-called 'neoclassical' production function. Neoclassical functions can take a host of forms (as we shall see in the following chapters) but they all have three fundamental characteristics. First they represent ways in which labour, capital and land can be combined to produce goods. Second, they assume that capital is a separate, independent input directly comparable with labour and land. And third, they focus attention on the production possibilities and decisions within processes, firms or industries.

Many of the results which spring from these functions, when applied to the various aspects of economics listed above, rely on these implicit assumptions. They are not without their critics.

A slightly different approach derives from general equilibrium models and focuses attention on *inter*-firm relationships of production. The Leontief production model is perhaps the best known example of this approach. Each sector uses capital and labour but also needs inputs from other sectors. The 'Food, Drink and Tobacco' sector, for example, buys materials from Agriculture, and Agriculture buys from Chemicals and so on. There is no substitution among inputs and so the inputs into each sector are usually assumed to be determined simply by the output of that sector. This approach is known as *input–output analysis* and concentrates on the interdependence of industries, firms and processes rather than choice of techniques within an industry, firm or process.

The input–output approach is widely used in planning models where the 'balance' among industries is important. And input–output is largely regarded as an alternative to neoclassical functions rather than a contradiction of them.

A third approach, the 'classical' production model, does however directly contradict the 'neoclassical' model. This approach is like the input–output approach in that attention is focused on inter-industry relations. In this classical model, however, one of the sectors produces capital goods – capital is explicitly recognised as a *produced* input. Whereas land and labour are 'original' inputs, capital is also an output. This modification is sufficient to render many of the 'standard' results of neoclassical production theory invalid. It is no longer unambiguously true, for example, that increasing the interest rate *vis-à-vis* the wage rate will induce capital saving. Sraffa (1972) has shown that it is possible for a particular man/machine combination to be used at low rates of interest, fall into disuse as interest rates rise and then, as they rise still further, switch back into operation again. This result would not be possible in a neoclassical model of production. As interest rate rises less and less capital is used and more and more labour so that the capital–labour ratio continues to fall for all increases in interest rate.

According to this classical model it is simply not possible simultaneously to determine factor and product prices as it is in the neoclassical world. It is necessary first to specify the wage/interest ratio and from this the choice of technique and product prices are found.

The so-called 'capital controversy' has been widely covered in the literature (Harcourt (1972), Kregel (1976) and cf. Bliss (1975)) and is rather beyond the scope of an introductory text such as this. Whatever merits or flaws the neoclassical production model may have it is indisputably the dominant model and economists require to have some understanding of it.

It is not our intention here to stress the controversies or to offer a comprehensive account of the various applications of production theory. Our aim is simply to bring together in one volume the principal neoclassical approaches to production and to compare and contrast their properties.

Production functions imply particular cost functions, often the 'self-dual' of the production function. These cost functions are sometimes of interest in their own right but are sometimes used as more tractable alternatives to production functions. For these reasons we introduce, where appropriate, the cost functions associated with each production function. We have tried to keep the inevitable mathematics to a fairly simple level and have consigned the more esoteric points to appendices which can be ignored by the general reader. Each chapter begins with fairly simple concepts and becomes progressively more difficult. Some students may find that the early parts of the chapters are all that is required.

There are two general chapters: one on estimating production functions and one on technological progress. These are included merely to indicate to the student some of the difficulties and some possible solutions which have been discussed in the literature.

We have, in short, tried to provide a rigorous yet accessible introduction to the principal aspects of cost and production functions.

*David F. Heathfield*
*Sören Wibe*

# Symbols

The following symbols are used throughout this book:

$q$ = Quantity of *firm output*.
$Q$ = Quantity of *industry output*.
$v_i, \ldots, v_n$ = *Firm inputs* No $1, \ldots, n$.
$V_1, \ldots, V_n$ = *Industry input*.
$K$ = Quantity capital (same for firm and industry).
$L$ = Quantity labour (same for firm and industry).
$E$ = Quantity energy (same for firm and industry)
$t$ = time.
$P$ = Prices of output (same for firm and industry).
$P_1, \ldots, P_n$ = Prices of inputs.
$\pi$ = Profits.
$\varepsilon$ = Elasticity of scale.
$\varepsilon_c$ = Elasticity of cost (with respect to production level).
$\sigma$ = Elasticity of substitution (in a two-factor production model)
$\sigma_{rs}$ = Allen partial elasticity of substitution between inputs $r$ and $s$.
$E_j$ = Price elasticity of demand for factor $j$.
$S_j$ = Cost-share for factor $j$.
$E_{ij}$ = Cross-price elasticity of demand for factor $i$.
$C$ = (Total) cost of factors.
$f_i$ = partial derivative of function $f(\ )$ w.r.t. factor $i$
$\xi_j$ = Input coefficient for factor $j$ (i.e. input per unit of output)
$U$ = Error term
$A, B, a, b, \alpha, \beta, \gamma, \lambda, \theta, \delta$ are used as parameters.

A dot ($\cdot$) above a symbol (e.g. $\dot{K}$) indicates *rate of growth*.

A line above a symbol (e.g. $\bar{q}$) indicates any arbitrarily fixed level.

A hat or a star above a symbol (e.g. $\hat{q}$ or $\overset{*}{q}$) indicates some special level (e.g. the cost-minimising level).

# Abbreviations

The following abbreviations are used throughout this book.

SR = Short Run
LR = Long Run

TC = Total Cost
FC = Fixed Cost
VC = Variable Cost
MC = Marginal Cost
AC = Average Cost
ATC = Average Total Cost ( = AC)
AVC = Average Variable Cost
AFC = Average Fixed Cost
LRAC = Long Run Average Cost
SRAC = Short Run Average Cost

TR = Total Revenue
MR = Marginal Revenue
AR = Average Revenue

TP = Total Product
AP = Average Product
MP = Marginal Product

RTS = Returns to Scale
CRTS = Constant Returns to Scale

DRTS = Decreasing Returns to Scale
IRTS = Increasing Returns to Scale

CD = Cobb–Douglas (Production Function)
CES = Constant Elasticity of Substitution (Production
    Function)

# Basic Concepts

## 1.1 Production

Production may be regarded as a transformation from one state of the world to another. But not all such transformations are acts of production. Consumption too may be regarded as a transformation from one state of the world to another.

In order to distinguish between them it is necessary to introduce the notion of preference. If the state of the world *before* transformation is preferred to that after transformation then transformation is an act of consumption. If, on the other hand, it were *not* preferred, then the transformation is an act of production.

Thus our preferences play a role in this rather basic classification and we simply have to decide for ourselves whether any particular transformation constitutes an act of production or an act of consumption. It is a subjective matter.

We can, however, define an act of production as any act which transforms the world from a less to a more preferred state.

### Acts of production

There are four ways in which the state of the world may be so changed:

(1) The *quantity* of a good may be changed: we can produce more motor cars for example;
(2) The *quality* of the good may be changed: we can produce better motor cars;

(3) The *geographical location* of a good can be changed: we can deliver a car to a customer;

(4) The *time location* of a good can be changed: we can hold a car in stock until the customer wishes to take delivery.

In the broadest sense then, production may be defined as any activity the net result of which is to increase the degree of compliance between the quantity, quality and distribution (spatial and temporal) of commodities and a given preference pattern. (Fixing the preference pattern rules out the possibility of increasing (or decreasing) production simply by changing tastes.)

In what follows we shall have little to say about the distributive trades and hence confine ourselves almost entirely to the first two types of production: changes in the quantity and changes of quality of goods and services.

## 1.2 Factors of Production

*Land* It is fairly obvious that, as we have defined them, acts of production can occur without the intervention of man. Salt water is transformed into fresh water, fruit and nuts grow and fish multiply in the seas and rivers without human involvement. All products so produced are the bounty of nature and have the generic name: *Land*.

*Labour* States of the world which result from purely natural processes do not always conform exactly with what we would wish. We have learned that by applying our human effort and intelligence to the natural processes we can bring about even better states of the world. By herding animals, by selecting certain seeds, by ploughing up the soil, we can produce more food of better quality. This input of human effort and intelligence is called *labour*.

Labour and land constitute the two primary *factors of production*. The latter provided free by nature and the former provided (often reluctantly) by human beings.

*Capital* There is, however, a third factor of production. It is a factor which has provoked, and continues to provoke, a great deal of controversy. We saw above that labour and land, separately or together, are capable of improving the state of the world. There is, however, no unique way of applying labour to land.

For example labour could scratch at the soil with finger-nails in order to prepare it for planting or labour could find and sharpen a pointed stick or could produce some iron for a spade or could produce a tractor and a plough in order to till the soil.

This sequence is in order of 'roundaboutedness' of the productive process. The first method, scratching with finger-nails, is very direct – one simply kneels down and gets on with it. The second requires a little time to be spent finding and sharpening the stick *before* tilling commences. The third method requires a great deal of work to be put in before one can actually begin tilling the soil. In other words the methods of production becomes more and more 'roundabout'.

This 'roundaboutedness' also turns out to be productive in the sense that when eventually it does result in 'tilling' it will till at a much greater rate than the more direct methods. It may, for example, take a day to find and sharpen a suitable stick. This would result in starting to till a day later than the scratcher. However, the man with the stick would soon overtake the scratcher and would eventually complete more tilling than he, the scratcher, would.

Roundaboutedness, being productive, is therefore another factor of production and is called *capital*.

The concept of roundaboutedness is not an easy one to grasp and many economists prefer to think of capital as all the land and labour which has been put into a productive process but which has not yet resulted in any consumable output. Thus, for example, a weaver of cloth may spend one year building a loom from two trees' worth of timber. At the end of that year he still has not produced any cloth (the consumable) but has produced a loom in readiness. His 'capital' then is his loom which is the physical embodiment of one year's labour and two trees.

At the end of that year he will begin weaving and feed thread into the loom. He must feed in quite a lot of thread and provide quite a lot of labour before he has a 'length' of cloth for sale. This thread and labour too, then, is capital in that it is land and labour currently within the productive process. Capital of this kind eventually emerges as the consumable and is replaced with new thread and more labour. It is therefore called *circulating capital*. Capital of the first kind (i.e. the loom) never emerges as a finished product and is called *fixed capital*.

In what follows we shall largely be concerned only with labour and fixed capital. We shall be interested in how labour and fixed capital can be used to improve the state of the world by changing the quantity and/or quality of goods available to us.

## 1.3 Factor Rewards

*Rent* It was claimed above that one factor of production, land, was provided free by nature. Nevertheless, as we shall see later, when used in production, land can attract a payment. This payment is called *rent* and derives partly from our institution of *private property*. Those who are deemed to 'own' oil wells, for example, can charge oil users for the crude oil even though the 'owner' had nothing whatever to do with its being there. Without private property natural endowments become 'free' goods as in the case of fresh air and sunshine. Free goods are of no interest economically, but the fact that some land attracts rent does influence production.

*Wages* Labour on the other hand is not a free good. In order for labour to engage in production it is necessary to forgo leisure – one must plough the land rather than lie abed! In order to persuade people to forgo their leisure it is necessary to recompense them in some way. This payment is called *wages*.

*Interest* The payment for capital is rather more complicated. We have seen that capital is a roundabout method of production and hence any payment for capital must be associated with the disutility associated with this roundaboutedness. This comes about in two ways. First the provision of capital requires someone, somewhere to do some work for no *immediate* reward, that is consumption must be postponed until the roundaboutedness is complete. Since most people prefer to consume now rather than later (positive time preference) they must be recompensed for their 'abstinence' and this payment is called *interest*.

*Profit* The second source of disutility associated with the provision of capital is that due to uncertainty about the future. The provider of capital has to put something into the process and then wait until some output is produced. During this waiting period almost anything could happen: the process might go wrong, the market conditions could change or the capitalist could expire. He therefore exposes his capital to *risk* and in order to persuade him to do so he is paid a *profit*.

Thus capital receives two types of payment: interest, which goes to those who abstain from immediate consumption (capitalists) and profit, which goes to those who bear the risk (entrepreneurs).

We have assumed that:

(1) Work, being forgone leisure, is something which people would rather not do.

(2) Waiting, being a denial of instant gratification, is something people would want to avoid.

(3) Risk is similarly something which people would wish to avoid.

None of these assumptions is obviously always correct – many people like their work, some people want to postpone consumption (e.g. for their retirement) and many people really like taking risks (gamblers). In the main, though, most people prefer the world as we assumed they would and if most people dislike their work, want immediate reward and are risk averse then any of these things will attract financial compensation in the form of wages, interest or profit.

## 1.4 Aggregation

*Factors* So far we have spoken of labour and capital as if there is only one kind of labour and one kind of capital. This is clearly a huge simplification. One man-hour of an unskilled labourer is not the same thing as a man-hour of a highly trained engineer. A certain amount of capital embodied in a loom is not the same thing as if it were embodied in a spinning machine.

Once the possibility of disaggregation is opened up it is difficult to see where it can logically end. The degree and nature of the disaggregation we choose to specify is once again a matter of judgement. Too much disaggregation leads to an infinitely long list of separate inputs and outputs. Too little masks significant differences between input (e.g. the skills of labourers).

In one way or another we have to rely on the *aggregation* of factors into some broad categories if we want to understand the process we study. The different kinds of labour used must be aggregated into one category (or possibly two categories) and the different kinds of machines have to be aggregated into one or two capital input measures. This aggregation is not without problems and will be analysed in greater detail later on in connection with macro production functions. Suffice it to say here that there is no clear principle as how to disaggregate each factor of production into its relevant subsets. It is simply a matter of common sense with classification depending on the purposes of the study and the data available.

*Output* Problems of aggregation are not confined to the input side of production. The output side also presents problems. If we define a 'plant' to be a production unit which produces one type of good of invariate quality, then we could measure the output of the plant by simply counting the number of goods produced. Unfortunately very few such 'plants' exist in practice. Most production units are 'firms' which produce a variety of goods with a variety of qualities. In the case of a farm, for example, how can we aggregate pigs, sheep, wheat and barley? In the case of a factory how can we aggregate cars with large engines, cars with small engines, cars with automatic transmission and cars with manual gearboxes?

For all these three, labour, capital and output, the aggregation problem falls into two stages. First deciding what constitutes a separate category, that is is it sensible to distinguish between skilled and unskilled workers, between workers who are under 35 years of age and those over 35? Is it sensible to distinguish between the number of blue cars produced and the number of red cars produced?

This first stage is a matter of judgement and depends upon the purpose of the study and the data available. Having decided which categories are relevant the second problem is how to combine the components of each separate category into a single number? This is the problem of index numbers.

*Index numbers* If, for example, it was decided that the appropriate category of output is 'corn', then the question remains as to how to aggregate wheat, barley and oats into this single measure called, generically, corn? One obvious possibility is to weigh each amount and simply add the weights together, that is 1 ton of wheat + 2 tons of barley + 4 tons of oats will equal 7 tons of corn.

Weight, however, is not always a good measure of output. Barley may weigh more than corn per cubic metre but the volume produced might be much more important than its weight. Typically in economics these problems are overcome by trying to find an *appropriate* and *common* characteristic which is numerical. In most cases this turns out to be value. Thus if wheat were twice as valuable as barley which in turn were twice as valuable as oats, then 1 ton of wheat + 2 tons of barley + 4 tons of oats would be equivalent to 3 tons of wheat, 6 tons of barley or 12 tons of oats.

An obvious problem here is that the actual number we come up with will depend on our units of measurement: it will be 3 tons if measured in wheat units and 12 tons if measured in oats units. One way around this is to measure it as a combination of all three inputs. Thus one unit of wheat is worth 2 units of barley or 4 units of oats then each 'basket' of output comprises:

$$\text{Output} = \frac{4}{7} \times \text{quantity of wheat} + \frac{2}{7} \times \text{quantity of barley}$$
$$+ \frac{1}{7} \times \text{quantity of oats.}$$

This output measure will still depend upon the units of measurement in the sense that if we switched from tons to kilogrammes we would have a different measure of output. One way around this is to divide the current year's output by the output of the 'base' year – year 0. This yields an *index* of output, thus:

$$\text{Index of output } 1 = \frac{\text{Output } 1}{\text{Output } 0}$$

$$= \frac{PW_0 QW_1 + PB_0 QB_1 + PO_0 QO_1}{PW_0 QW_0 + PB_0 QB_0 + PO_0 QO_0}$$

that is Index of output $1 = \left( \dfrac{PW_0 QW_0}{VO} \right) \left( \dfrac{QW_1}{QW_0} \right)$

$$+ \left( \dfrac{PB_0 QB_0}{VO} \right) \left( \dfrac{QB_1}{QB_0} \right) + \left( \dfrac{PO_0 QO_0}{VO} \right) \left( \dfrac{QO_1}{QO_0} \right)$$

where $VO = PW_0 \times QW_0 + PB_0 \times QB_0 + PO_0 \times QO_0$

$PW_0$ = price of wheat in period 0
$QW_0$ = quantity of wheat in period 0
$QW_1$ = quantity of wheat in period 1
$PB_0$ = price of barley in period 0
$QB_0$ = quantity of barley in period 0
$QB_1$ = quantity of barley in period 1
$PO_0$ = price of oats in period 0
$QO_0$ = quantity of oats in period 0
$QO_1$ = quantity of oats in period 1

The index of output is therefore *non-dimensional* since it is completely independent of any *unit* of measurement whether we use tons or kilogrammes, francs or pounds. The change in the quantity of each element ($Q_1/Q_0$) is multiplied by the value of that element ($P_0 Q_0$) divided by the total value of output ($VO$) in a chosen base year (year '0').

Thus each input is multiplied by a number representing its importance in terms of value. These numbers are called 'weights' and since in this case they are based on the relative values they are called value weights.

This measure of aggregate output would rise by only 1/7 of a unit if we produced 1 ton more oats but would rise by 4/7 of a unit if we produced another ton of wheat. Notice too that if we produce an extra ton of each of wheat, barley *and* oats, then aggregate output would rise by 1 unit that is the value weights sum to unity.

Obviously the values of wheat, barley and oats will change over time. Barley may become more valuable than wheat for example. Thus we have to decide which values to use. If we choose the values of a particular historic date (1970) then we have a *Laspeyre* (L) index. All we need to compile such an index is the relative prices of wheat, barley and oats in one particular year and their tonnage thereafter.

Conversely, we could use the latest (current) values and thus compile a *Paasche* (P) index. In this case of course it becomes necessary to know the current prices whenever the index is being compiled. Thus the 1980 index used 1980 prices but the 1984 index uses 1984 prices.

Unfortunately, neither of these indexes is *ideal*. For example, if we used either L or P to measure the change in output between 1980 and 1984 we would get different measures depending on whether we measured *from* 1980 *to* 1984 or *from* 1984 *back to* 1980. They do not in other words satisfy the *time reversal condition*.

*Fisher's Ideal Index Number* (F) does satisfy the time reversal condition and is a geometric mean of the Paasche and Laspeyre index numbers. Thus:

$$F = \sqrt{L \times P}$$

## Processes

So far we have considered aggregation *across* various types of labour, of capital and of output. There is, however, a further problem of aggregation and it is to do with the aggregation of a sequence of processes. This can be illustrated by taking the case of steel production.

The production of steel requires capital and labour and iron and could be regarded as a single production process – the steel production process. The iron producing process itself uses iron ore and iron ore is 'produced' by applying capital and labour to the land (mining). Thus there is yet another process which precedes the iron producing stage.

These three stages are illustrated in Figure 1.1.

**FIGURE 1.1**

| Process 1 Mining | | Process 2 Iron production | | Process 3 Steel production | |
|---|---|---|---|---|---|
| Inputs | Output | Inputs | Output | Inputs | Output |
| Capital Labour Land | Iron ore | Capital Labour Iron ore | Iron | Capital Labour Iron | Steel |

A study of steel production could regard all these three stages as a single process moving from the mine to steel. In this case there would be three inputs, capital, labour and land and one output, steel.

Alternatively, steel production could be regarded purely as stage 3. In this case the inputs would be capital, labour and iron and output would be steel.

Thus each of these separate stages (and any *sequential* combination of them) (1 + 2, 2 + 3, 1 + 2 + 3) could be regarded as a process.

There are two points to note here. First the stages of production are linked by the flow of commodities from one stage to the next. These commodities are called *single use intermediates*. They are, like capital, a *produced* input into a stage of production but unlike capital they do not persist for more than one period. Once used they have to be replaced. Thus they are 'single use' rather than durable.

Second, each stage in the production of steel is independent in that it has its own labour and its own capital. The capital and labour introduced at each stage adds its contribution to the production of the ultimate output–steel. This contribution made by capital and labour at each stage is called the *value added* and is equal to the value of its output (*gross output*) less the value of its single use intermediates.

The value of steel will therefore be equal to the value added at stage 3 plus the value of iron. The value of iron will be the value added at stage 2 plus the value of iron ore. The value of iron ore will be the value added at stage 1 plus the rent on the mine.

Thus the value of steel is the sum of the value added at each of the three stages plus rent.

Production is analysed sometimes in terms of the inputs of capital and labour and their value added, sometimes in terms of inputs of capital and labour and gross output, sometimes in terms of inputs of capital, labour and single use intermediates and gross output. In each case, however, it is customary to focus attention on the inputs and outputs of some aggregate of stages, that is of some process.

A rather different approach is one which focuses attention on the interdependence of the stages of production. Thus for example it would be important to know not only how much capital was engaged in the production of steel but also how it was distributed among the various stages. This interdependence approach is based on the work of Leontief and is called *input–output* or *inter-industry analysis*.

## 1.5 Varying Inputs and Outputs

An important aspect of the theory of production is the choice of a particular process and the choice to produce particular quantities of output. The use of the word 'choice' implies that there are some alternatives available, that is some flexibility in the use of inputs and in the quantity produced.

The quantity currently being produced can of course be reduced should the need arise – the process could even be closed down if necessary. Reducing output typically means reducing some or all of the inputs. The input of intermediates could swiftly be reduced but the labour force and the capital stock are not quite so conducive to rapid reduction. In the case of labour there are contracts of employment restricting the discretion of the employer. In the case of capital the problem is even more severe. If the firm has bought its capital then it can be disposed of only through a second-hand market usually at a considerable loss.

Thus there are costs associated with the rapid reduction of labour and capital. Cost which the employer may seek to avoid, or minimise, by not responding immediately to all reductions in demand for his product. He may produce for stocks or he may allow some men and machines to lie idle for a while.

The opposite case is one in which demand increases. Here again it may be possible to quickly obtain larger inputs of intermediates but increasing employment and capital cannot be achieved overnight. Demand may be met from stock or by working the existing capital and labour more intensively by operating overtime.

Thus the variability of output and inputs is not always costless and rapid. Some inputs are more flexible than others in the sense that their cost of change is low. If change is allowed to take place slowly enough then adjustment costs fall to some irreducible minimum. If, for example, a machine has a 'life' of ten years, then a decision to scrap it in year nine is much less costly than a decision to scrap it in year two. In year ten the scrapping is free since it has no value anyway. Similarly, if the labour contract requires one month's notice of dismissal, then the reduction of the labour force over a month's duration will be free compared with the cost of immediate dismissal.

The variability of inputs is therefore a function of the time period. The *short run* will be regarded as the time period in which everything but capital can be adjusted costlessly but in which full capital costs cannot be avoided. The *long run* will be regarded as the time period in which all factors can be adjusted at minimum cost.

The *time period* of our study is accordingly an important aspect and must be carefully specified. But a classification of factors as fixed or variable is nevertheless somewhat arbitrary. Let us assume for instance that we wish to study production conditions in a firm and that we fix the period of production as 3 months. Assume now that we find that the firm can costlessly change its use of intermediates by $\pm$ 100 percent during this period. Labour stock can change by $\pm$ 20 percent and capital stock by a maximum of + 10 percent. It is obvious that intermediates are a variable factor here and that capital can be perhaps safely regarded as fixed. But what about labour? Every decision here is difficult and somewhat arbitrary. A classification of factors into fixed and variable is, at best, only an approximation of real conditions.

## 1.6 The Production Function

The production function is the core concept in the economic theory of production. We have analysed production processes as the means of transforming certain inputs (capital, labour, land and intermediates) into certain outputs (cars, bread, steel, etc.). It is clearly absolutely critical to know how much output can be produced with certain combinations of inputs and what, if any, alternatives there are to producing particular outputs in particular ways. The production function is an attempt at defining these alternatives. It is, in other words, an attempt at mathematically specifying the range of technical possibilities open to producers. This needs to be qualified slightly since we are not interested in wasteful processes – processes which use more of any input than is absolutely necessary. Thus the production function is the set of possible *efficient* relations between inputs and outputs given the current state of technological knowledge.

We now introduce a formal definition of the production function. Imagine a process where only one (homogeneous) output is produced. We denote the quantity of this output by $q$. Assume also that output is produced with '$n$' homogeneous factors of production and denote the quantities of these $v_1, \ldots, v_n$. The dimensions of $q$ and $v_1$ are *units per time period*, that is they are what we call *flow units*.

We can now formally write our production function

$$q = f(v_1, \ldots, v_n) \tag{1:1}$$

where $f(\quad)$ denotes the *form* of the production function.

The form of the production function depends on the technology of the process. We could, for instance, have an *additive* production function:

$$q = a_0 + a_1 v_1 + a_2 v_2 \ldots + a_n v_n \tag{1:2}$$

with $a_0, \ldots, a_n$ being constants. Or the production function could have the little more complicated *multiplicative* form:

$$q = a_0 v_1^{a_1} v_2^{a_2}, \ldots, v_n^{a_n} \tag{1.3}$$

(Several other forms do, of course, exist and form the subject of succeeding chapters.)

The interpretation of (1), (2) or (3) is simple: given a flow of inputs $v_1, \ldots, v_n$ we can produce a flow of output $q$, provided we use the most efficient technology. (By deliberate waste of resources, we can, of course, always produce less than $q$.)

The production function, at least as defined originally, is a *micro* concept. It applies to production relations within the smallest economic unit: a process, a firm, or a plant. It is furthermore a purely technical relation which can be constructed without any reference to market conditions or prices. It represents the choice set. Economic aspects enter only when it comes to choosing one of these possible input–output configurations.

## 1.7 The Isoquant

A most useful way of picturing the production function is by way of the *isoquant*. (Iso = equal, quant = quantity). The idea is that a given amount of output can be produced with many different factor combinations. For instance, when digging a ditch we can either use several men with spades or we can use one man and an excavator. The former means that we use a very labour-intensive technology, the latter that we use a capital-intensive technology. The isoquant is a way of representing these technological possibilities. Consider, for simplicity, a process with only two factors of production, labour ($v_1$) and capital ($v_2$). Assume also that we hold output constant, $q = \bar{q}$. We then have a relation:

$$\bar{q} = f(v_1, v_2) \tag{1.4}$$

where only $v_1$ and $v_2$ are allowed to vary. The range of combinations allowed by (1.4) is the isoquant for the production level $q = \bar{q}$. Two such isoquants (one for $\bar{q}$ and one for $\bar{\bar{q}}$) are illustrated in Figure 1.2.

Any combination of labour and capital on isoquant 1 is capable of a producing output $\bar{q}$. At point A a great deal of labour and very little capital is being used. At point C a lot of capital and a little labour produces the same output. A is therefore said to be more labour intensive than C and C is said to be more capital intensive than A.

At some higher level of output ($\bar{\bar{q}}$) more labour and/or more capital is required. There will be one isoquant for each level of output so that this $v_1$ $v_2$ space is dense with isoquants none of which touch or cross any other.

As drawn these isoquants are strictly convex from above, that is a straight line joining any two points on an isoquant will everywhere lie above the isoquant. We shall see later what shapes of isoquant are deemed possible. For the moment we will simply state that convexity is the most common assumption.

**FIGURE 1.2**
**Two Isoquants in the Two-factor Case**

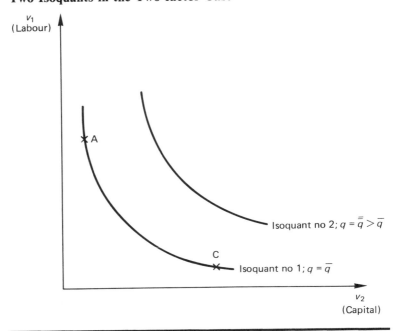

## 1.8 Homothetic Production Function

We pointed out earlier that many forms of the production function are possible. However, most of the production functions used in empirical analyses are *homothetic* functions. The definition of a homothetic production function can be explained in terms of its isoquants. All such functions (and no other class of functions) have isoquants that are radial projections of each other. This is illustrated in Figure 1.3.

In Figure 1.3, the isoquant for $q = \bar{\bar{q}}$ is only a 'blown up' version of the isoquant $q = \bar{q}$. The slope of the isoquants are preserved along every ray through the origin, that is the isoquant slope at A equals the slope at B. And that at C equals that at D. It is also easy to show that this implies that BA/BO = DC/DO.

**FIGURE 1.3**
**The Isoquants of Homothetic Production Functions**

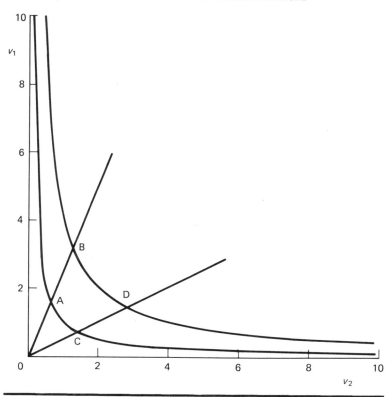

## 1.9 Technological Progress

The production function, and the corresponding isoquant map, has been defined as representing *one state of technology*. Advancements in technological knowledge therefore leads to shifts in the production function so that more output can be produced with a given set of inputs. This again can be conveniently analysed with the isoquant map. Consider Figure 1.4.

**FIGURE 1.4**
**Illustrating Technological Progress with the Isoquant**

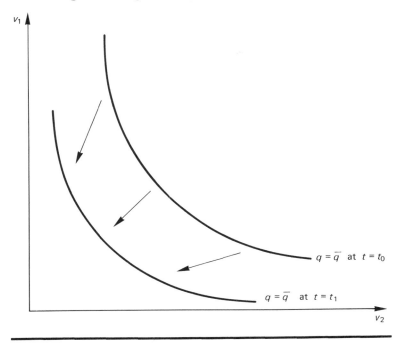

Figure 1.4 illustrates one isoquant at two different points of time, $t_0$ and $t_1$. If technological progress has occurred between $t_0$ and $t_1$ this means that more can be produced at $t_1$ with the same amounts of inputs than at $t_0$. This is the same as saying that fewer inputs are needed to produce the same amount of output, that is that the isoquants have moved towards the origin. Such a movement is displayed in Figure 1.4. In this figure we have illustrated a case where the isoquant has moved rather uniformly towards the origin, but this need not be the case. Progress can, for instance, imply that factor saving only occurs for one factor of production, for example labour. In this case the isoquant would have moved downwards, parallel to the labour axis and technological progress would be *biased* in the labour-saving direction.

## 1.10 Returns to Scale

Changes in scale result from movements from one isoquant to another rather than from movements along a particular isoquant. To increase the scale of production it is necessary to increase each of the inputs without changing their proportions. Thus the increases in inputs must be equiproportionate. A 10 percent increase in labour, for example, and a 10 percent increase in capital represents a 10 percent increase in inputs.

Scale properties are key characteristics of a production function and can be illustrated with the density of the isoquant map. Changes in scale are movements along a ray radiating from the origin of the isoquant map. This is shown as line 0A in Figure 1.5.

**FIGURE 1.5**
**The Isoquant Map and Returns to Scale**

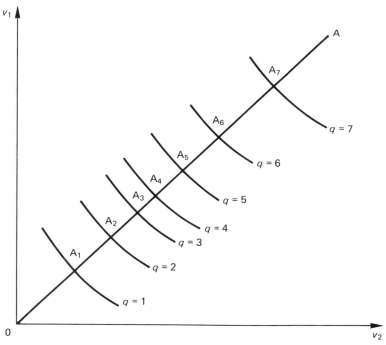

The seven isoquants represent seven levels of output and where they cut the ray $0A(A_1-A_7)$ they represent output changes due to changes in scale. The ratio $A_2/A_1$ is the proportionate increase in inputs necessary to increase output from $q = 1$ to $q = 2$, that is to double output. If $A_2/A_1$ is less than 2 it means that we can double output without doubling inputs. This is called *increasing returns to scale*. If $A_2/A_1$ is exactly 2 then we need twice the quantities of inputs in order to produce twice the amount of output. This is called *constant returns to scale*. If $A_2/A_1$ is greater than 2 then we have to more than double the quantities of inputs in order to double output. This is called *decreasing returns to scale*.

As we move along the ray we may move from a range in which we experience increasing returns into a range in which returns are constant and thence into a range in which returns are decreasing.

Assume now that we produce one unit ($q = 1$) with the amounts of labour and capital as indicated by $A_1$. From Figure 1.5 we can see that the distance $OA_1$ is greater than $A_1A_2$. This means that we need not double inputs in order to double output. Similarly, we see that $A_1A_2$ is greater than $A_2A_3$ which means that increasing output from one to two units demands proportionately more inputs than increasing output from two to three units.

From Figure 1.5 we see that increasing output by one unit demands proportionately less and less of inputs up to the level $q = 4$. After that, one additional unit of output demands proportionately more and more of inputs. This is the same as saying that factor productivity increases up to $q = 4$ and decreases thereafter or that the process exhibits *increasing returns to scale* in the interval 0–4 (units of output) and *decreasing returns to scale* for output levels greater than four units. Transforming this to the isoquant map we might say that increasing returns to scale means that the isoquant map becomes more and more dense as output grows, while the opposite is true for decreasing returns.

*Note* *Constant* returns to scale does not imply *invariate* returns to scale. Returns to scale can change from constant to increasing or to decreasing as we move along the ray.

## 1.11 Factor Substitution

Whereas changes in scale were concerned with movements from one isoquant to another, factor substitution is to do with movements along an isoquant. The isoquants reveal the possibilities of factor substitution for a process. The same quantity can be produced with many alternative combinations of labour and capital.

The possibilities of factor substitution are revealed by the *curvature* of the isoquants. Three different cases are illustrated in Figure 1.6. In Figure 1.6(a), we have the case of a fixed technology. It is obvious that only the factor combination represented by point A is efficient since all other points on the isoquant use more of one factor, *but not less of the other* to produce the same output. The opposite extreme (to Figure 1.6(a)) is represented by Figure 1.6(b). Here we have unlimited possibilities of substitution since one unit of factor $V_1$ can always be substituted for some units of factor $V_2$. In Figure 1.6(c) we have the normal case of factor substitution. Substitution is always possible, but it becomes increasingly more difficult to substitute one unit of factor $v_1$ for factor $v_2$ as we move from a $v_1$ intensive choice to a $v_2$ intensive choice.

## The Isoquant in the Long and the Short Run

Imagine that we want to start the production of a product and that one step in the preparation of this is the construction of the relevant isoquant map. This results in the Figure 1.7 which shows all the possible factor combinations for the process in question. But the combinations refer to the possibilities when we have a free choice of all inputs. This would be the case *before* we made the investment or in the *long run* when we can redesign the plant. Therefore before the investment or in the long run, we can regard every factor as variable and look at Figure 1.7 as the relevant description of the technical possibilities open to us.

But assume that we have made the fundamental investment and that the factory is built. If we then analysed the technical possibilities in the short run, we would have to take various restrictions into account. The amount of capital invested would be fixed and not possible to increase. It is also probable that there would exist a lower limit to the use of capital (at positive production) since we must use all the buildings etc. even if only a small amount of output is produced.

For labour, we assume that we could decrease the number of employees to any desired level, but the design of the factory may prevent us from using more than $L_{max}$ persons. (After that we assume

20

**FIGURE 1.6**
**The Isoquant and Factor Substitution**

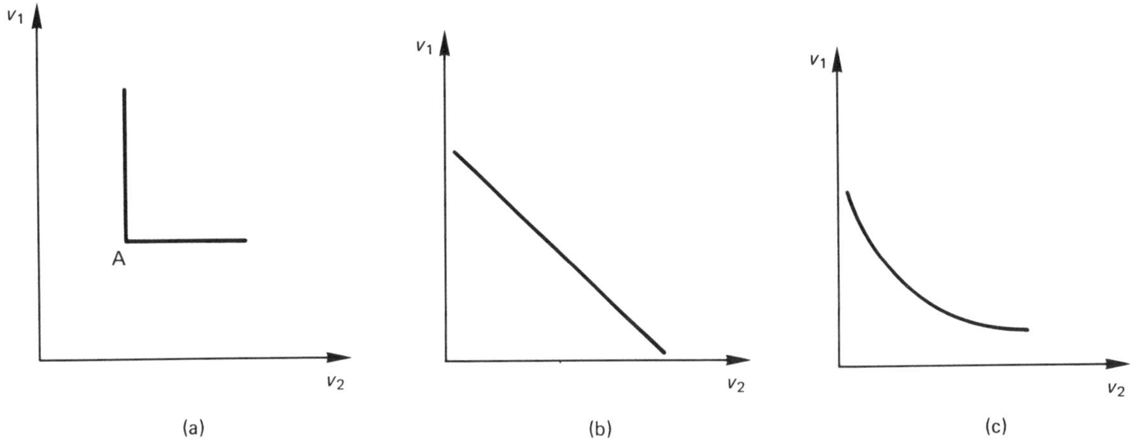

(a)

(b)

(c)

**FIGURE 1.7**
**Long-run Isoquant Map**

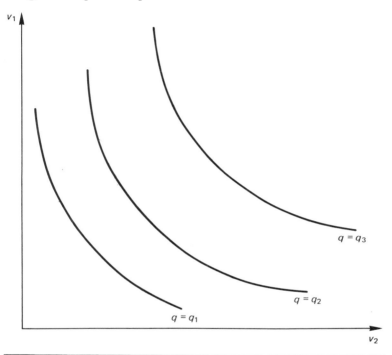

that the factory becomes so crowded that total production actually decreases with an addition labour.)

Thus, the *range* of substitution between capital and labour would decrease as a result of all these restrictions. The substitution possibilities could be quite different before and after the investment. Before the investment it could be possible to substitute £100 worth of capital for 1 man, but after the investment, when all our pounds are frozen as concrete buildings and machines, it may 'cost' £500-worth of capital goods to substitute one man.

The reasoning above leads to the conclusion that we cannot in general derive the short run isoquants from the long run map. This relation depends in all cases on the concrete technical details. The illustration of short-run isoquants given in Figure 1.8 will therefore serve only as an illustration of a possible case.

**FIGURE 1.8**
**The Short-run Isoquant Map**

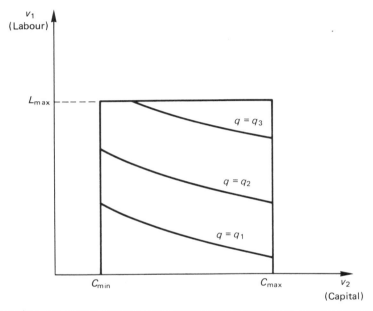

## 1.12 Total, Average and Marginal Products

So far we have represented the production function as an isoquant map but there are alternative representations, one of which is closely associated with the theory of the firm. This alternative approach relies on the total, average and marginal product curves.

### Long Run

In the long run when all inputs are variable we can show how total output grows as the level of inputs increases (in fixed proportion). This is shown in Figure 1.9.

**FIGURE 1.9**
**Total Output Curve**

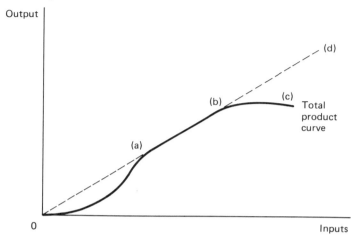

As inputs increase from (0) to (a) output is increasing faster than inputs and hence there are increasing returns to scale. Between (a) and (b) the total product curve runs along a ray through the origin (0) (d) and hence a 10 per cent increase in inputs leads to a 10 per cent increase in output and is therefore a range of constant returns to scale. Beyond point (b) output increases slower than inputs and hence is a range of decreasing returns.

The long-run *average* product curve can be derived from this by simply dividing the output by one of the inputs. (Since all inputs change in proportion any input would do.) This long-run average product curve is shown in Figure 1.10.

Average product is rising between (0) and (a)–the increasing returns to scale range. It is constant between (a) and (b) with CRTS and falls beyond (b) where there are DRTS.

## *Short Run*

In the short run we require at least one input to be fixed and hence can define total, average and marginal product curves in terms of the

**FIGURE 1.10**
**Average Product Curve**

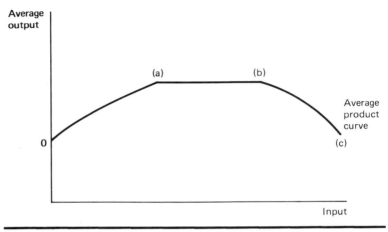

variable factor(s). Assuming a production function:

$$q = f(v_1, v_2)$$

and assuming that one input is fixed; $v_2 = \bar{v}_2$, we can derive a relation between the quantity of $v_1$ and total output. This relation; $q = f(v_1, \bar{v}_2)$ is called the total product curve and will of course depend on the chosen value of $v_2$. Two total product curves, corresponding to two values of $\bar{v}_2$, are illustrated in Figure 1.11–below. With $\bar{v}_2$ units of $v_2$ output increases as $v_1$ increases. With more of $v_2$, say $\bar{\bar{v}}_2$, more output is produced for any input of $v_1$ and hence the total product curve for $\bar{\bar{v}}_2$ lies everywhere above that for $\bar{v}_2$.

The average product (AP) of one factor of production is defined as output per unit of that input. The average product of a factor will of course depend on the chosen value of the fixed factor. Two AP curves for $v_1$, corresponding to two different values of $v_2$, are illustrated in Figure 1.12.

The average product of labour ('labour productivity') is often used as an index of the efficiency of a process. But the average product of one factor does of course, as Figure 1.12 shows, depend on the use of all other factors. Thus, a process with high labour productivity may

**FIGURE 1.11**
**Two Total Product Curves**

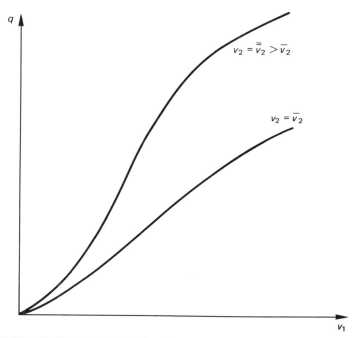

very well be technically inefficient in that it uses great quantities of capital. In order to estimate the overall efficiency of a process, we must take into account the use of all inputs, not only one.

The *marginal product* (MP) of a factor is defined as the increase in output resulting from *one additional unit* of the factor. Assuming that a small change in $v_1$ ($\Delta v_1$) results in a change in output of $\Delta q$, we define the marginal product of $v_1$, ($MP_1$) as

$$MP_1 = \Delta q / \Delta v_1 \tag{1.5}$$

More formally we define $MP_1 = \delta q / \delta v_1$.

Like the total and the average product curves the shape of the marginal product curve also depends on the amount of the other factor(s) available.

The shape of the marginal product curve is something to which

**FIGURE 1.12**
**Two Average Product Curves**

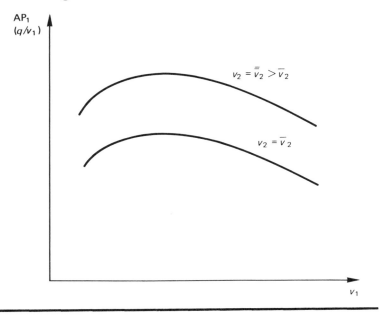

economists have traditionally attached a great deal of importance. The central concept is that of The Law of Diminishing Returns.

## 1.13   Diminishing Returns

The law of diminishing returns states that if more and more of a variable factor is applied to a fixed quantity of other factors, then eventually the resulting increases in output must diminish. Thus the marginal product curve must eventually slope downwards.

There are two ways in which this law may be justified. The first relies on the heterogeneous nature of the 'fixed' input. In the early stages of production only the most suitable bits of the fixed input will be in use but as output expands the producer is forced to use more of the least suitable bits of fixed inputs and hence the increments in output become less and less. This is the case in agriculture in which the fixed input is land and the variable input is labour. At first only the most productive land is used and labour is highly productive. Eventually as output expands worse and worse land is pressed into service so that the productivity of the last labourers is less than that of the first.

This law of diminishing returns is that of the *extensive* margin.

The second type of explanation relies not on the heterogeneity of the fixed input but upon the idea of an 'optimum' proportion of factors. If the variable input is less than that which is regarded as 'optimal' given the quantity of fixed input, then as it increases it will become more productive. Thus up to the optimum point the marginal product will be increasing. Beyond that point, however, the marginal product will be decreasing as the factor proportions become less and less 'optimal'. This is the so-called *intensive margin*.

The importance of this distinction, between extensive and intensive margins, derives from the effect they have on rent. Rent is the reward paid to landowners and occurs in classical theory from the fact that land at the extensive margin yields less than land within the margin. Thus those who own land within the margin can charge 'rent' equal to the excess production per acre of their land over that at the margin. If land in the valley yields 10 tons of wheat per acre per man and if land on the hillside yields 5 tons of wheat per acre per man then the valley land attracts rent to the value of 5 tons of wheat. Thus rent occurs when different yields are concurrently being reaped. It will not occur therefore when dealing with the intensive margin. Working all homogeneous land more intensively will decrease productivity everywhere equally and hence there will be no land yielding more than any other. The possibility and cause of rent will not therefore arise.

## Selected Reading

An informative background to the study of production theory is given in J. Schumpeter, *History of Economic Analysis* (1954), Chapters 6 and 7. The history of the production function is treated separately in section 7.8. An introduction to the basic concepts of production is given in R. Frisch, *Theory of Production* (1965) chapters 1–4, and a shorter overview is given in C.E. Fergusson, *The Neoclassical Theory of Production and Distribution* (1969), Chapters 1–2.

The law of diminishing return was first discussed by two classical economists: Ricardo (1846) and von Thünen (1826). But see also Joan Robinson (1960).

# Cost Functions and the Theory of the Firm

## 2.1 Optimisation

Having outlined the range of choices open to an entrepreneur (the production function), we shall now investigate the economic side of production, that is the choice of a technology and a level of output from among the many possible.

The fundamental decision unit here is the firm, and we will assume that the firm's sole aim is to maximise profit. Profit is defined as the difference between total revenue (TR) and total cost (TC).

Possible profits will be determined partly by market conditions (i.e. prices of factors and output) and partly by the technological choice set represented by the production function. The problem for the firm is therefore to choose: (i) A scale of output (i.e. an isoquant) and (ii) A particular technology (i.e. a point on the isoquant) such as to maximise profits. We shall analyse these two aspects in the context of a simple two-factor model.

## 2.2 The Isocost Line

Let us assume that the prices of our two inputs, $v_1$ and $v_2$, are fixed at $P_1$ and $P_2$ respectively. Total cost, TC, is then

$$TC = P_1 v_1 + P_2 v_2 \tag{2.1}$$

An isocost line is a line representing all combinations of $v_1$ and $v_2$ which can be purchased for a particular sum of money, at a constant (ISO) total cost, $TC = \overline{TC}$.

Such combinations can be found by rearranging equation (2.1):

$$v_1 = -(P_2/P_1)v_2 + \overline{TC}/P_1 \tag{2.2}$$

which is an equation for a straight line in the $v_1, v_2$ space and is drawn in Figure 2.1

**FIGURE 2.1**
**The Isocost Line**

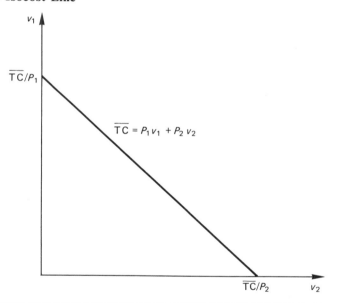

The *slope* of this isocost line is

$$dv_1/dv_2 = -P_2/P_1 \tag{2.3}$$

and the *intersections with the axes* are $\overline{TC}/P_1$ and $\overline{TC}/P_2$.

A higher level of total costs would shift the isocost line outwards from the origin leaving the slope unchanged. Only a change in the ratio of factor prices would alter the slope.

## 2.3 The Cost-minimising Choice of Technology

A choice of technology is a choice of a point on an isoquant and since we are interested in the choice of a point on an isoquant we shall assume that the level of output has been fixed, $q = \bar{q}$. Total revenue (which equals product price times output, $TR = P.\bar{q}$) is then also fixed, and the maximisation of profits is equivalent to the minimisation of costs. The firm will therefore choose a point on the given isoquant which minimises costs. *The problem is therefore to choose from all the points on the isoquant, the point with the corresponding isocost closest to the origin.* This problem is illustrated in Figure 2.2.

**FIGURE 2.2**
**The Cost-minimising Choice of Technology**

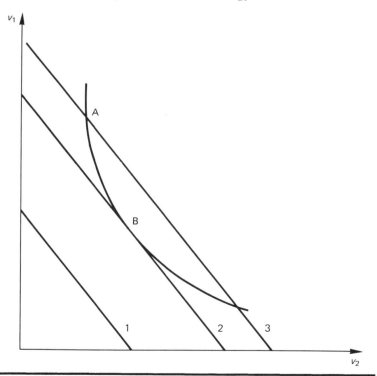

The isoquant and three different isocost lines are displayed in Figure 2.2. We can see immediately that the isocost line 1, though lowest, is irrelevant since it has no point (factor combination) in common with the isoquant. It is therefore impossible to produce the required output at the cost represented by isocost line 1. It is, however, possible to produce with the factor combination represented by point A since that point does lie on the isoquant. But point A is associated with the isocost line 3 and we can see that the cost would be lower at point B (on isocost line 2).

It is evident that B represents the cost-minimising solution since every isocost line representing a lower cost (closer to the origin) does not have a common point with the isoquant. We can therefore conclude that cost minimisation requires the isocost line to be tangential to the isoquant, that is a point at which:

> The slope of the isoquant
> equals
> the slope of the isocost

We know from the analysis above that the slope of the isocost line equals $-P_2/P_1$. What about the slope of the isoquant? Taking the total differential of the production function $q = f(v_1, v_2)$ yields:

$$dq = f_1 dv_1 + f_2 dv_2 \qquad (2.4)$$

where $f_i$ is the marginal product of factor $i$ ($MP_i$ or $\delta q / \delta v_i$). But if we are constrained to move along an isoquant (i.e. hold output constant), then $dq = 0$. We can accordingly solve (2.4) for $dv_1/dv_2$ (the isoquant slope):

$$dv_1/dv_2 = -f_2/f_1 \qquad (2.5)$$

Thus, our condition for cost minimisation in the two-factor case becomes $P_2/P_1 = dv_1/dv_2 = f_2/f_1$, i.e.

$$P_2/P_1 = f_2/f_1 \qquad (2.6)$$

We shall accordingly choose that point on the isoquant where *the ratio of the marginal products $(f_2/f_1)$ equals the ratio of factor prices $P_2/P_1$*.

## Changing Input Prices

A change in input prices changes the slope of the isocost line and alters the profit maximising solution. For instance, an increase in the price of $v_2$ leads to a steeper isocost and a less $v_2$–intensive technology becomes optimal. We characterise this change of technology as a *substitution process*. In Figure 2.3, the increase in $P_2$ leads to the choice of the technology represented by B instead of A. Factor $v_2$ is substituted for factor $v_1$ in proportions $\Delta v_2 / \Delta v_1$.

**FIGURE 2.3**
**The Effects of Changing Input Prices. $P_2$ Increases**

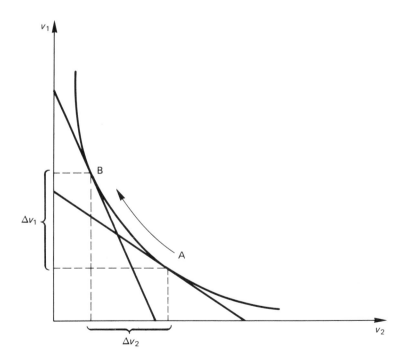

## 2.4   Cost-minimising Choice of Technology in the Short Run

The analysis in the preceding section can be regarded as the long-run choice of technology since both factors vary without any restrictions. Assume now that the fundamental investment has already been made and that we want to analyse the choice of technology in the *short run*. In the short run, capital represents a 'sunk cost' and the firm has to pay interest and mortgages even if the equipment is left idle. As a simplification, we shall assume that *the ex post* (the 'user') *cost of capital is zero*. Of course the possession of capital still involves costs, but the cost difference between using and not using the equipment is zero, so the *use* of existing capital stock may be regarded as free. The cost structure facing the firm in the short run is therefore quite different from that of the LR case.

If $v_2$ represents capital, we can now write the short-run cost function; SRTC

$$SRTC = FC + P_1 v_1 \tag{2.7}$$

$(TC = P_2 v_2 + P_1 v_1$ but $P_2 v_2$ is fixed)

where FC represents the *fixed cost* of production. For a given value of SRTC, equation (2.7) can be interpreted as the short-run isocost line.

Some SR isocost lines and an isoquant are shown in Figure 2.4. In this case the minimum cost is not zero but equal to the fixed cost. Thus the minimum isocost line equals fixed cost and lies on the $v_1$ axis between 0 and $\bar{v}_2$. This is because the firm can employ no labour but can employ any quantity of capital between zero and $\bar{v}_2$, for nothing more nor nothing less than fixed cost. A somewhat higher isocost line would permit some labour to be hired and this labour could be combined with any quantity of capital between 0 and $\bar{v}_2$. Thus this isocost line too is horizontal between the $v_1$ axis and $\bar{v}_2$.

The firm would again wish to minimise costs for its given level of output and would hence choose that isocost line closest to the $v_2$ axis and which touches the isoquant.

The isocost closest to the origin (with one point in common with the isoquant) is displayed in the figure (Isocost 2).

The cost minimising solution implies obviously, as Figure 2.4 shows, that all the existing capital stock is utilised. This solution minimises labour input and, as a consequence, minimises the variable costs of production.

**FIGURE 2.4**
**LR Isoquant and SR Isocost Lines**

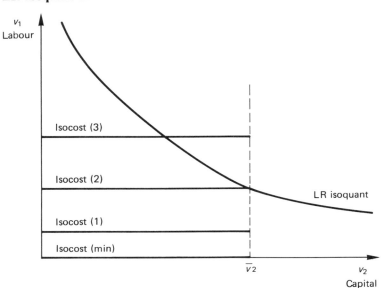

## 2.5   Cost Functions in the Long Run

Long-run analysis implies that both factors are allowed to vary. For every isoquant we could obtain the cost minimising point $v_1^x \cdot v_2^x$ and by connecting all these points (for one specific price ratio $P_2/P_1$) find an *expansion path* (see Figure 2.5).

There will be one expansion path for each price ratio. For a homothetic production function the expansion paths are straight lines going through the origin (which means that *factor proportions, $v_1/v_2$* remain unchanged unless input price ratios change).

Thus, for each output level and set of input prices we can calculate a minimum level of total costs. Thus, we have a unique relation between output, input prices and (the minimum of) total costs:

$$TC = H(q, P_1, P_2) \tag{2.8}$$

which is the *cost function*.

**FIGURE 2.5**
**The Expansion Path**

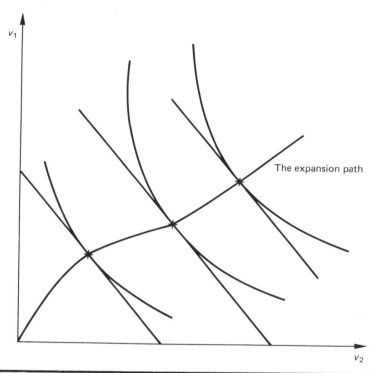

The expansion path

This function has a very simple form if the production function is homothetic since the cost function is then multiplicative separable, with one term involving only $q$, and the other the input prices: $TC = H^q(q) . H^P(P_1, P_2)$.

All cost functions are *homogeneous of degree 1 in the input prices*, that is doubling all prices leads to a doubling of total costs. This is natural since a doubling of all (in this case both) prices does not alter the slope of the isocosts and does not change the cost-minimising input combination at a specific isoquant. With $v_1, v_2$ unchanged and a doubling of $P_1, P_2$, it is obvious that $TC = P_1 v_1 + P_2 v_2$ must double.

Equation (2.8) refers to total costs. The *average total cost*, ATC, is obtained by dividing by $q$:

$$ATC = TC/q \tag{2.9}$$

Since all factors are variable in the long run, we have an identity between *total* and *variable* cost. Thus, ATC = AVC, where AVC = average *variable* costs.

The *marginal cost* (MC) is the increase in total costs following a unit increase in output. Using the derivative notation:

$$MC = \frac{dTC}{dq} \tag{2.10}$$

By holding input prices constant, we can study the variation of cost with output. The shape of the cost functions do of course depend on the underlying production function, and in particular, its scale properties. Assume that the production function has the shape which is indicated in the isoquant map in Figure 1.5. At first we have a phase with increasing returns to scale and later on a phase with decreasing returns. Inspection of Figure 1.5 shows that this leads to a total cost curve with first a decreasing slope and then an increasing slope. Such a total cost curve is illustrated in Figure 2.6 below. The average and marginal cost curves derived from this total cost curve (Figure 2.6) are displayed in Figure 2.7. The marginal cost is simply the *slope* of the TC curve at any point (dTC/dq) and the AC is the slope of a line connecting any point on the TC curve to the origin (TC/$q$).

Both the AC and the MC curves are U-shaped (cf. the inverted 'U'-shaped average and marginal product curves). This is not an unnatural property from a technical point of view. Most processes have large scale economies, meaning that average cost of production declines initially. However, it seems reasonable to assume that average cost must start to increase somewhere. Transportation costs, costs of managing a very large organisation, lack of flexibility for very large firms, etc. are some of the factors which are put forward to explain why increasing economics of scale eventually will come to an end and why average production costs eventually increase. It must, however, be remembered that the point where average costs start to increase may be at a very large output level, perhaps many times larger than the largest existing firm.

The MC curve in Figure 2.7 intersects the AC curve from below and at the minimum of AC. This is always the case. The MC curve must be

**FIGURE 2.6**
**The Total Cost Curve**

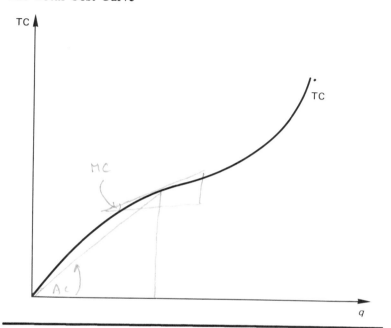

located beneath the AC curve if the latter is falling and above the AC curve when the latter is rising. Accordingly, the MC curve must intersect the AC curve at its minimum point as in Figure 2.7.

Mathematically we have:

$$TC = AC \times q$$

$$MC = \frac{dTC}{dq} = AC + \frac{dAC}{dq} q$$

Therefore

$$\frac{dAC}{dq} q = MC - AC$$

Hence the slope of AC is positive when $MC > AC$ and negative when $MC < AC$.

**FIGURE 2.7**
**Average and Marginal Cost Curves**

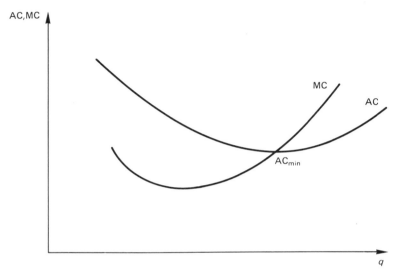

## 2.6   Cost Functions in the Short Run

The general form for short-run cost functions is~~is~~ given in equation
(2.7). The important difference between short- and long-run cost
functions is that only the former has a fixed component. Assume that
we wish to calculate the cost-minimising solution for each possible
output level. We would then obtain a short-run cost function:

$$\text{SRTC} = H_{SR}(q, P_1) \tag{2.11}$$

The short-run cost curve has few properties in common with the
long-run curve. A doubling of $P_1$ will not, in general, lead to a
doubling of costs, and the equation is not multiplicative separable in $q$
and the input prices even if the original production function is
homothetic.

The short-run cost function (2.11) consists of a fixed and a variable
part. We shall assume that the variable part increases with output
firstly at a decreasing rate and then an increasing rate, exactly like the

total cost curve in Figure 2.6. (This assumption is based on the law of diminishing returns.)

In addition we assume that the variable cost curve becomes vertical at a point $q = q_{max}$. This assumption is natural since given our short-run situation there must exist an absolute limit to output – a *physical capacity ceiling*. Economically, this ceiling implies that the cost curves are vertical.

The short run average and marginal cost curves can now be constructed (Figure 2.8). Since total costs now have a fixed component, we must distinguish between average total costs, ATC, and average variable costs, AVC. The average cost curves in Figure 2.8 are U-shaped, just like the long-run average cost curves in Figure 2.7. Observe that the distance between AC and AVC becomes smaller as output increases. Since AFC equals a fixed cost divided by output, it

**FIGURE 2.8**
**Cost Curves in the Short Run**

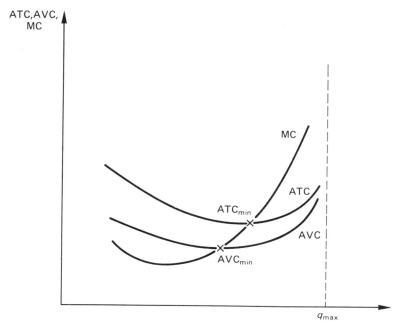

must approach zero as output grows and AVC must accordingly approach ATC.

We observe also that the minimum of AVC occurs at a rate of output lower than the minimum of ATC and, of course, that the value of $AVC_{min}$ is lower than $ATC_{min}$. Note also that the marginal cost curve intersects with the AVC and the ATC curves at their minimum points.

The minimum SR average total cost is the 'capacity' point. *Note* This is the economic capacity (the design point) of the plant. It is not the 'physical' capacity level.

## 2.7   The Relation Between Long- and Short-run Cost Curves

The relation between the long- and the short-run cost curves is similar to the relation between the long- and short-run isoquant map. The essential difference is that capital in the long run is completely variable, whereas capital in the short run is fixed. Since variability in the long run is always superior to variability in the short run it is not surprising that the short-run cost curves never fall below the long-run cost curves.

Consider Figure 2.9. The LRAC curve (Long-run Average Cost Curve) shows how long-run (minimum) costs change with output with given input prices. It represents the very best that can be done given the current state of knowledge.

If the plant is designed to produce $q_1$ units of output the minimum average cost would be $AC_1$. That is the cheapest possible way of producing $q_1$. *Note* Average costs could be further reduced by slightly expanding output above $q_1$. Both the long-run and the short-run cost curves are downward sloping at that point. Obviously the LR curve falls more sharply than the SR curve. However, these cost advantages can only be gained by *increasing output beyond* $q_1$. $AC_1$ may not be the lowest point on any average cost curve but it is the lowest cost for producing that particular quantity $q_1$.

When the LRAC curve flattens out – that is there are constant returns to scale – the minimum cost of producing $q_2$ will be at the lowest points of both the LRAC curve and the SRAC curve.

There will be a short-run average cost curve for each point on the LRAC curve and since no SRAC curve can fall below the LRAC it follows that the LRAC curve is the envelope of all the short-run cost curves.

**FIGURE 2.9**
**Long- and Short-run Average Cost Curves**

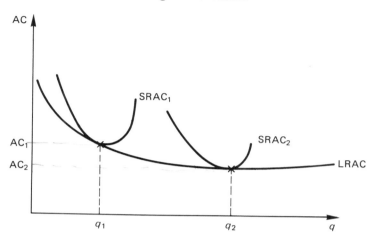

## 2.8   Factor Demand in the Long and Short Run

We have seen that, for a given level of output, the choice of factor
proportions will be uniquely determined by their relative prices.
Relative factor prices determine the cost minimising point on the
specified isoquant and hence determine how much capital and how
much labour will be used in the production process.

The firm's demand for factors of production is therefore a function
of the rate of output and relative input prices. Formally these *factor
demand functions* can be written:

$$v_1 = g_1(q, p_1, p_2)$$
$$v_2 = g_2(q, p_1, p_2) \tag{2.12}$$

It will be apparent from the isoquant–isocost diagram that factor
demands are not affected by price *level* but only by price *ratios*. Thus
doubling all prices leaves the factor demand unchanged, that is
equations (2.12) are homogeneous of degree zero in prices.

Furthermore, if the isoquants are those of a homothetic function
then equations (2.12) are multiplicative separable in output and

prices, that is doubling output will double the demand for all inputs if relative prices remain unchanged.

In the short run all but one input is 'fixed' and it was demonstrated above (Figure 2.3) that the firm will always choose to make maximum use of the fixed factor. Thus in the short-run factor prices play no part in the factor demand functions. At these corner solutions the variable input will be a function of output only.

## 2.9   Determination of Output Level

We have so far assumed that the level of output was given. Our task in this section is to analyse how the optimal level of output is determined. Since we have assumed that the firm has only one aim: to maximise profits, the optimal level of output is the same as the level which maximises profits.

The firm's profit $(\pi)$ is the difference between total revenue (TR) and total costs (TC). Thus:

$$\pi = \text{TR} - \text{TC} \tag{2.13}$$

For $\pi_{\text{max}}$ the firm must choose the $q$ for which $d\pi/dq = 0$ and $d^2\pi/dq^2 < 0$.

$$\frac{d\pi}{dq} = \frac{d\text{TR}}{dq} - \frac{d\text{TC}}{dq} = 0$$

that is

$$\frac{d\text{TR}}{dq} = \frac{d\text{TC}}{dq} \tag{2.14}$$

that is marginal revenue equals marginal cost.

The second order condition for a max is:

$$\frac{d^2\pi}{dq^2} < 0$$

and

$$\frac{d^2\pi}{dq^2} = \frac{d}{dq}\left(\frac{d\text{TR}}{dq}\right) - \frac{d}{dq}\left(\frac{d\text{TC}}{dq}\right)$$

that is

$$\frac{d^2\pi}{dq^2} = \frac{dMR}{dq} - \frac{dMC}{dq} \tag{2.15}$$

It is obvious that MR curves will rarely slope upwards. They would be horizontal ($dMR/dq = 0$) for perfect competition and negative for monopolist firms. Thus if the MC curve is upward sloping the second order conditions will be satisfied. An upward sloping MC curve could arise from decreasing returns to scale or due to factor prices rising as output grows. Problems begin to emerge when there are constant or increasing returns to scale. Under perfect competition and constant returns to scale the MC curve is horizontal and hence $dMC/dq$ is 0.

Thus with perfectly competitive markets for input and output and with constant returns to scale both $dMR/dq$ and $dMC/dq$ equal zero and the second order conditions for a maximum *are not satisfied*.

These points are made more rigorously in the mathematical appendix to this chapter.

Both the MR and the MC curves can be said to consist of two parts: one direct (quantity) effect and one indirect (price), effect. Whether or not the second effect is big depends on the firm's size relative to the total market. If the firm is the sole seller on the market (monopoly) it is reasonable to assume that the product price is affected by a change in output. Similarly, if the firm is the sole buyer on a factor market (monopsony) we may assume that the factor price is affected. If, on the other hand, the firm is very small compared with the total market for the product and for the factors we might safely assume that all prices are unaffected by the firm's decision on output level (perfect competition). In that case we might regard all prices as constants.

The determination of output level does accordingly depend on the firm's market for factors and on the product market. In the rest of this chapter we shall consider output determination under two extreme conditions: monopoly and perfect competition. We totally disregard the price effects on the factor markets, and assume that the firm cannot influence the price of its factors.

## 2.10 Output Determination in Perfect Competition

We assume now that the firm operates in a market characterised by perfect competition. Among other things, this means that the firm is small compared with the size of the total market for the product, and that it cannot influence market price by changing its output. If the firm charges a price below that of the market, it can sell all it can produce. If, on the other hand, the firm charges a price above that of the market, it will discover that its sales are zero. Thus, *the firm faces a horizontal demand curve in perfect competition.* The aggregate demand curve for the product (the demand curve for the whole industry) is of course downward sloping, and if all firms acted together, they would be able to change the price by changing output. But since one firm is so small compared with the market, a change in output for one firm will have virtually no effect on market price.

Let us first consider the problem of output determination *in the long run.* Since markets are characterised by perfect competition, we know that the MR curve equals product price, $P$. (The extra revenue from the sale of one additional unit is its price.) From Figure 2.7 we obtain the shape of the long-run ATC and MC curves, and we can illustrate the problem with the figure 2.10 below.

**FIGURE 2.10**
**Output Determination in Perfect Competition: Long Run**

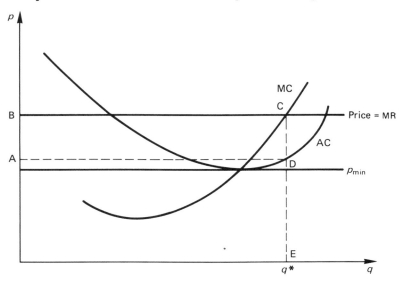

Profit is maximised if the firm produces $q*$ because this is the level where MC = MR. At $q*$, the firm obtains a price amounting to EC for each unit, while at the same time its unit's costs are ED. Accordingly, the firm makes a profit amounting to DC for each unit which makes a total profit of ED $\cdot q*$ (which equals the size of the rectangle ABCD in Figure 2.10).

If the firm expects that $P$ is to be the long-run market price it will build a factory designed for a capacity of $q*$. But the existence of positive profits will draw new capital to the industry and more firms will be established. This process will force the price down in the long run.

This process will continue until the price has fallen to $P_{min}$. The establishment of any new firm will thereafter lead to a market price below the lowest possible cost, and all firms will then make losses. Ultimately, this will lead to the closing of some firms, and the price will increase to $P_{min}$ again. This process of firms entering and leaving is the reason why it is assumed that the long-run equilibrium price yields zero profits and why production occurs at the point of constant returns to scale (i.e. flat bit of the LRAC curve). It must be remembered, however, that our reasoning is based on many simplifying assumptions. First, we assume that technology is fixed, so that the cost curves do not shift. Second, we assume that all prices are fixed. None of this may be true in the long run. Technology and prices move constantly, leading to a constant changing of cost curves. The process described above should therefore not be understood as a total description of market behaviour, but as the description of *one very important element* in the behaviour of markets. The character of this behaviour does not change even if some details in the exposition are altered. Competition in the sense of firms entering and leaving, and the connected pressure on market price, is according to all empirical evidence a very important element in the behaviour of market economies. What we have learned here is that the central organising concept of long-run equilibrium is a zero profit point. It is *achieved* by firms seeking to maximise profits in markets with free entry.

Let us now look at the problem in the short run. Assuming a constant price ($=$ MR) and the cost curves as represented by Figure 2.8 (reproduced in Figure 2.11, below), we have the situation shown in Figure 2.11.

The character of the solution is the same as in the long run. The firm will produce $q*$ because at $q*$ we have MR = MC. Total profit at this

**FIGURE 2.11**
**Output Determination in Perfect Competition: Short Run**

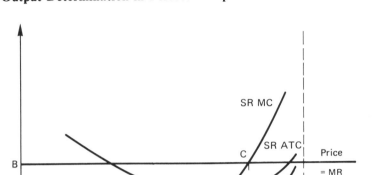

level is $(EC - ED) \cdot q^* =$ the area ABCD.

The difference between the long and short run is: (a) there is no entry and (b) the reaction to price falling below minimum average total cost is not always to close down. In the short run the firm will continue producing until the price falls below the AVC curve. This is because the firm has to pay the fixed costs whether it produces or not, hence the firm will find it profitable to go on producing *as long as it can cover its variable costs.* As long as the price is higher than AVC, the firm can obtain some contribution to its fixed costs by producing. However, when the price falls below $AVC_{min}$, the act of producing leads to avoidable losses, and the firm will close. *Thus, only the variable cost matters in the short run.* The short run supply curve in perfect competition is therefore that part of the MC curve which lies above the SRAVC curve.

## 2.11  Output determination in a Monopolistic Market

We shall now consider output determination under monopoly. Monopoly means that a single firm supplies the market and that the *firm's demand curve is the market's*. The firm will accordingly face a downward sloping demand curve and will have to consider the price-effects of changing its level of output. The demand curve is the *average revenue curve* since it shows how much the firm gets *on average* for each unit of production at each level of output. The MR curve will be *below* the demand curve, because the extra revenue coming from an additional unit of sales will be lower than the price. An additional unit will force price down not only for the extra unit but also for all other units. The marginal revenue of that unit must accordingly be lower than its price.

For simplicity, we shall consider the case with a linear demand curve. We assume that a monopoly faces a demand curve with the equation

$$P = a_0 - a_1 \cdot q \tag{2.16}$$

where $a_0$, $a_1$ are constants ($a_0 > 0$, $a_1 > 0$).

This is a straight line from the point $a_0$ on the $P$-axis to the point $a_0/a_1$ on the $q$-axis.

The equation for the MR curve can be obtained from (2.16).

$$\text{MR} = \frac{\partial \text{TR}}{\partial q} = \frac{\partial (a_0 q - a_1 q^2)}{\partial q} = a_0 - 2a_1 q$$

which is a straight line from the point $a_0$ on the $P$-axis to the point $a_0/2a_1$ on the $q$-axis. (Note the MR curve has twice the slope of the AR curve but the same intersect.) Using the long-run cost curves from Figure 2.7, we obtain Figure 2.12.

Profit maximisation implies the production of $q^*$ units, because at $q^*$, MR = MC. For this quantity the firm obtains the price $p^*$. The average cost of production at $q^*$ is ED, and total profits accordingly equal to the area ABCD.

Monopoly is here assumed not to alter the cost curves which remains the same as it was in the case with perfect competition. Neither does it alter the market's demand curve or the profit maximising condition MR = MC. What happens is that the firm's MR curve no longer equals the demand curve. This in turn leads to lower production and higher price than in the perfectly competitive

**FIGURE 2.12**
**Output Determination in a Monopolistic Market. Long Run**

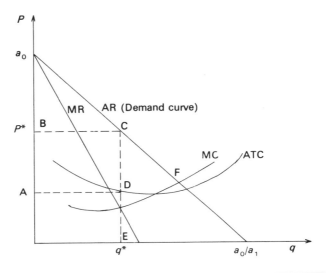

situation. (Perfect competition would lead to a MC being equated with the market AR curve at F.)

In this case it is assumed that no competitor can enter and bid away the profits. Thus the central organising concept here is profit maximising rather than the inevitability of zero profits.

Even if the firm is operating at a point of increasing returns to scale the second order conditions may still be satisfied by the negatively sloped demand curve.

## Appendix: Returns to Scale, Imperfect Markets and the Second Order Conditions for a Maximum

Profits is defined as:

$$\pi = Pq - Cq \tag{A2.1}$$

where $P$ is average revenue and is a function of $q$ and $C$ is average cost and is a function of $q$.

For a max $d\pi/dq = 0$ hence:

$$\frac{d\pi}{dq} = \frac{\partial P}{\partial q} q + P - \frac{\partial C}{\partial q} q - C = 0 \tag{A2.2}$$

or

$$P\left[\frac{\partial Pq}{dq \cdot P} + 1\right] = C\left[\frac{\partial C}{\partial q}\frac{q}{C} + 1\right] \tag{A2.3}$$

but $\partial pq/\partial qP$ is the elasticity of the demand curve for the product, $Ep$ and $\partial c \cdot q/\partial q \cdot C$ is the elasticity of costs with respect to output $Ec$. For constant returns to scale $Ec = 0$, for increasing returns to scale $Ec < 0$ and for decresing returns to scale $Ec > 0$. For all normal demand curves $0 > Ep > -1$.

Thus for perfect competition ($Ep = 0$) and constant returns to scale ($Ec = 0$) (A2.3) implies that average revenue ($P$) equals average cost ($C$) and hence is the condition for zero profits. For constant returns to scale and imperfect competition $P > C$ and positive profits are possible. Similarly for decreasing returns to scale and perfect competition.

This is implied by the second order conditions for a maximum, that is $\partial^2\pi/\partial q^2 < 0$. Thus from (A2.2) we have:

$$\frac{\partial^2\pi}{\partial q^2} = \frac{\partial^2 P}{\partial q^2} q + 2\frac{\partial P}{\partial q} - \frac{\partial^2 C}{\partial q^2} q - 2\frac{\partial C}{\partial q} < 0 \tag{A2.4}$$

For simplicity assume that returns to scale do not change as output changes (i.e. $\partial^2 C/\partial q^2 = 0$). Further assume that the demand curve is a straight line (i.e. $\partial^2 P/\partial q^2 = 0$). (A2.4) then becomes:

$$2\frac{\partial P}{\partial q} - 2\frac{\partial C}{\partial q} < 0$$

or

$$\frac{\partial P}{\partial q} < \frac{\partial C}{\partial q} \tag{A2.5}$$

Thus for increasing returns to sale $[(\partial C/\partial q) < 0]$ the second order condition for a maximum requires imperfect competition $[(\partial P/\partial q) < 0]$ and for perfect competition $[(\partial P/\partial q) = 0]$ it is necessary to have decreasing returns to scale $[(\partial C/\partial q) > 0]$.

Equation (A2.5) therefore defines all combinations of returns to scale and imperfect competition for which the second order conditions are satisfied.

In more general terms let

$$q = f(v_1, v_2) \tag{A2.6}$$

$$P = F(q) \tag{A2.7}$$

$$\pi = Pq - p_1 v_1 - P_2 v_2 \tag{A2.8}$$

As conditions for maximum we have $\partial \pi / \partial v_i = 0$, *thus:*

$$F_1 f_1 q + P f_1 = P_1 \tag{A2.9}$$

and

$$F_1 f_2 q + P f_2 = P_2$$

or

$$f_1 \left( \frac{F_1 q}{P} + 1 \right) = \frac{P_1}{P} \tag{A2.10}$$

and

$$f_2 \left( \frac{F_1 q}{P} + 1 \right) = \frac{P_2}{P}$$

which are the marginal productivity conditions, where

$$F_1 = \frac{\partial P}{\partial q} \quad \text{and} \quad f_i = \frac{\partial q}{\partial v_i} \tag{A2.11}$$

*Note:* $F_1 q / P$ = elasticity of price with respect to quantity $(1/Ep)$ and when there is perfect competition $1/Ep = 0$ and

$$f_1 = \frac{P_1}{P}, f_2 = \frac{P_2}{P} \tag{A2.12}$$

In order for these first-order conditions to imply a max rather than a min it is necessary that $d\pi^2 < 0$ and

$$d^2\pi = (F_{11} q + 2F_1)(f_1^2 dv_1^2 + 2f_1 f_2 dv_1 dv_2 + f_2^2 dv_2^2)$$
$$+ (F_1 q + P)(f_{11} dv_2^2 + 2f_{21} dv_1 dv_2 + f_{22} dv_2^2) \tag{A2.13}$$

where $F_{11} = \partial^2 P / \partial q^2$

If we assume a straight line demand curve then $F_{11} = 0$, also, since demand curves slope downwards, we know that $F_1$ is -ve.

Equation (A2.13) can therefore be written:

$$d^2\pi = 2F_1(f_1\,dv_1 + f_2\,dv_2)^2$$
$$+ (F_1q + P)(f_{11}\,dv_1^2 + 2f_{21}\,dv_1\,dv_2 + f_{22}\,dv_2^2) \qquad (A2.14)$$

The first term of (A2.14) is unambiguously negative. As to the second term of (A2.14) we have two parts. The first part is:

$$(F_1q + P) = P\left(\frac{F_1q}{P} + 1\right) = P(Ep + 1) \qquad (A2.15)$$

Since the demand elasticity must always be negative it follows that (A2.15) is unambiguously positive ($-1 > Ep > \infty$ implies negative marginal revenue). The sign of (A2.14) therefore depends on the sign of:

$$(f_{11}\,dv_1^2 + 2f_{21}\,dv_1\,dv_2 + f_{22}\,dv_2^2) \qquad (A2.16)$$

which in matrix notation, is:

$$[dv_1, dv_2]\begin{bmatrix} f_{11} & f_{12} \\ f_{12} & f_{22} \end{bmatrix}\begin{bmatrix} dv_1 \\ dv_2 \end{bmatrix} \qquad (A2.17)$$

Therefore for $d^2\pi$ to be unambiguously negative (A2.16) has to be negative (i.e. the matrix of (A2.17) must be negative definite).

To see how the sign of (A2.16) depends on the elasticity of scale, consider the generalized Euler equation:

$$q\varepsilon = f_1v_1 + f_2v_2 \qquad (A2.18)$$

where $\varepsilon$ is the elasticity of scale.

Differentiating (A2.18) w.r.t. $v_1$ and $v_2$ yields:

$$\left.\begin{array}{l} f_1\varepsilon = f_{11}v_1 + f_1 + f_{21}v_2 \\ f_2\varepsilon = f_{12}v_1 + f_2 + f_{22}v_2 \end{array}\right\} \qquad (A2.19)$$

and

Multiplying the first term of (A2.19) by $v_1$ and the second by $v_2$ and summing yields:

$$\varepsilon(f_1v_1 + f_2v_2) = f_{11}v_1^2 + f_1v_1 + f_{21}v_2v_1 + f_{22}v_2^2$$
$$+ f_2v_2 + f_{12}v_1v_2 \qquad (A2.20)$$

But $f_1v_1 + f_2v_2 = q\varepsilon$, and $f_{21} = f_{12}$, therefore:

$$\varepsilon(q\varepsilon) - (q\varepsilon) = f_{11}v_1^2 + 2f_{21}v_2v_1 + f_{22}v_2^2 \qquad (A2.21)$$

therefore

$$q\varepsilon(\varepsilon - 1) = f_{11}v_1^2 + 2f_{21}v_2v_1 + f_{22}v_2^2 \tag{A2.22}$$

The RHS of (A2.22) is the same as (A2.16) hence substitution in (A2.14) yields:

$$d^2\pi = 2F_1(f_1\,dv_1 + f_2\,dv_2)^2 + P(\varepsilon_p + 1)(q\varepsilon(\varepsilon - 1)) \tag{A2.23}$$

From (A2.23) we have that

(a)   $d^2\pi < 0$ when $F_1 < 0$ and $\varepsilon \leqslant 1$, i.e. with imperfect competition and either constant ($\varepsilon = 1$) or decreasing ($0 < \varepsilon < 1$) returns to scale.

(b)   $d^2\pi = 0$ when $F_1 = 0$ and $\varepsilon = 1$, that is perfect competition and constant returns to scale.

(c)   $d^2\pi > 0$ when $F_1 = 0$ and $\varepsilon > 1$, i.e. perfect competition and increasing returns to scale.

Increasing returns to scale can be tolerated if there is sufficient imperfection of the product market, that is the second term in (A2.23) may be positive but could be overcome by a large negative first term.

This argument is strengthened if $F_{11}$ is also negative rather than zero since if $F_{11}q < -P$ then increasing returns to scale would not upset the second order conditions. The demand curve is falling even faster and must eventually cut the average cost curve no matter how the cost curve falls provided it does so at a constant rate.

## Selected Reading

Comprehensive statements of the theory of the firm can be found in S. Carlsson, *A Study on the Pure Theory of Production* (1939); S. Dano, *Industrial Production Models* (1966); R. Frisch, *Theory of Production* (1965) and in C.E. Fergusson, *The Neoclassical Theory of Production and Distributions* (1969). The duality between cost and production functions are stated in P. A. Samuelson, *Foundations of Economic Analysis* (1947) and in R. W. Shephard, *Cost and Production Functions* (1953). The theory of monopoly and imperfect competition was developed in J. Robinson, *The Economics of Imperfect Competition* (1933). The difference between short and long run is clearly exposed in W. E. G. Salter, *Productivity and Technical Change* (1960) and L. Johansen, *Production Functions* (1972).

# Elasticity, Efficiency and the Theory of the Firm

**3**

## 3.1 Introduction

In this chapter we shall ignore technological progress and focus attention on two quantitative aspects of a static production function. The first concerns some useful tools for investigating the relationship between prices and choice of technologies. The interface as it were between the technical and the economic aspects of production.

The second concerns the assumption of efficiency. It is clear that not all firms in an industry would be operating at maximum efficiency all the time. Our observations of the real world will not therefore always lie on the 'frontier' of production possibilities.

## 3.2 Output and Substitution Effects

In order to investigate the relationship between prices and the choice of technology we confine our attention (at least for the moment) to a two-factor production function:

$$q = f(v_1, v_2)$$

Each factor has its own price $P_1$ and $P_2$ respectively and the ratio of these prices will determine the choice of technology (i.e the point on the isoquant). If the price of factor 1 is increased from $P_1$ to $P'_1$, then this will lead to two effects:

(i) Factor 1 would become relatively more expensive than factor 2 and thereby cause factor 2 to be substituted for factor 1.

(ii) The total cost of producing any given level of output would increase because one input is now more expensive.

The first effect is called the *substitution effect* since at any given level of output factor 2 is substituted for factor 1. The second effect is called the *output effect* since for any given level of *costs* the amount of output which can be produced is reduced.

These two effects are illustrated in Figure 3.1.

---

**FIGURE 3.1**

**Illustrating the Effects of an Increase in the Price of Factor 1, $P_1$ to $P_1'$ with Constant Total Cost TC**

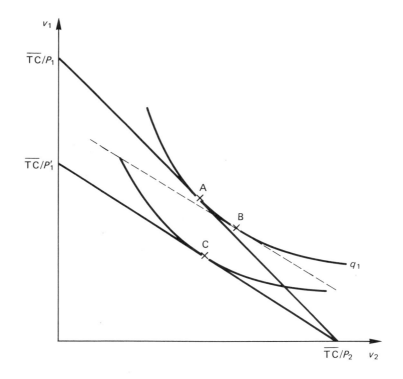

---

We assume that the firm produces $q_1$ with the technology indicated by A and with total cost equal to $\overline{TC}$. An increase in $P_1$ to $P'_1$ changes the optimum point *at a constant level of total cost* to C which, obviously, is on a lower isoquant. Thus we conclude that a particular level of cost is associated with a lower level of production or, which is the same, that every level of production is now associated with a higher level of costs as a factor price increases.

The change between A and C involves both a change of output and a change of factor proportions. Let us, however, try to separate these effects by analysing the change in factor proportions at a constant level of output. To regain the original output after the price change, we move the new isocost line parallel with itself until it touches the original isoquant $q_1$, that is to the point B. The change between A and B can now be defined as the substitution effect since it shows the change in factor proportions in response to a change in factor prices but with output held constant. The change between B and C can in a similar fashion be defined as an output effect, since it shows the reduction in output necessary if total costs are to remain unchanged.

## 3.3 The Elasticity of Scale

The extent to which changing cost-curves will affect equilibrium output level will, obviously, depend on the *shape* of the cost curves.

The relevant economic measure here is *the elasticity of scale*. The elasticity of scale is the ratio of the proportionate increase in output to the proportionate increase in inputs. If we assume that both inputs increase by the same percentage so that $dv_1/v_1 = dv_2/v_2 = dv/v$, we can define the elasticity of scale by the equation:

$$\varepsilon = (dq/q)/(dv/v) \tag{3.1}$$

($dq/q$ is the proportionate change in output resulting from the change in inputs.)

An alternative expression for $\varepsilon$ can be derived from a production function $q = f(v_1/v_2)$. If we differentiate the production function we obtain:

$$dq = f_1 dv_1 + f_2 dv_2 \tag{3.2}$$

where $f_1 = \partial q/\partial v_1$ and $f_2 = \partial q/\partial v_2$ (3.2) can be rewritten:

$$(dq/q) = f_1 . (dv_1/v_1) . v_1/q + f_2 . (dv_2/v_2) . v_2/q \tag{3.3}$$

But, since $dv_1/v_1 = dv_2/v_2 = dv/v$, we obtain:

$$(dq/q) \, / \, (dv/v) = f_1. \, (v_1/q) + f_2. \, (v_2/q) \tag{3.4}$$

But $(dq/q) \, /(dv/v) = \varepsilon$ and hence

$$\varepsilon = f_1. \, (v_1/q) + f_2. \, (v_2/q) \tag{3.5}$$

which formula can easily be generalised to the case with $n$ factors of production:

$$\varepsilon = \sum_{i=1}^{n} f_i. \, (v_i/q) \tag{3.6}$$

where $f_i = (\partial q/\partial v_i)$. From (3.1) we have that for $\varepsilon = 1$, doubling all inputs will lead to a doubling of output. This case is referred to as *constant returns to scale*.

If $\varepsilon < 1$, then doubling inputs will lead to a less than doubling of output, a case which is called *decreasing returns to scale*.

If, finally, $\varepsilon > 1$, doubling all inputs will lead to a more than a doubling of output and we speak of *increasing returns to scale*.

There is a strong empirical case for assuming that most industrial processes exhibit increasing returns to scale, that is that the elasticity of scale is greater than 1 for most output levels. This is one of the most important causes of industrial concentration, and the analysis of the scale properties of production functions constitute therefore an important element in studies of this important trend.

However, the elasticity of scale is certainly not the only parameter determining the size of the firms in an industry. Many other factors, such as corporate strategies, distance to the market and the raw material sources, relation between the firms and the industry's market, etc., are all important too. The elasticity of scale of the production function is but one factor determining the size structure of an industry.

## 3.4  The Elasticity of Scale and Shape of the Cost Functions

As intuitively described in Chapter 1, there is a close relation between the cost curves and the scale properties. This relation is easiest to see if we introduce the elasticity of cost, $E_C$. The elasticity of cost is the ratio of the (relative) increase in cost to the (relative) increase in output. If total cost is denoted C (earlier TC), we define:

$$E_C = (dC/C)/(dq/q) \tag{3.7}$$

Furthermore:

$$E_C = 1/\varepsilon \tag{3.8}$$

that is the elasticity of cost is the reciprocal of the elasticity of scale.

*Proof.* We have that: $C = P_1v_1 + P_2v_2$
where $C$ is total cost.
    Therefore $dC = P_1dv_1 + P_2dv_2$
    Therefore

$$dC = v_1P_1\frac{dv_1}{v_1} + v_2P_2\frac{dv_2}{v_1}$$

for scale changes we have that

$$\frac{dv_1}{v_1} = \frac{dv_2}{v_2} = \frac{dF}{F}$$

    Therefore $dC = dF/F \ (v_1P_1 + v_2P_2)$

but $v_1P_1 + v_2P_2 = C$

    Therefore $dC/C = dF/F$

dividing both sides by $dq/q$ yields

$$\frac{dC}{C} \cdot \frac{q}{dq} = \frac{dF}{F} \cdot \frac{q}{dq}$$

The RHS is $1/\varepsilon$ and the LHS is $E_C$
    Therefore $E_C = \dfrac{1}{\varepsilon}$

Thus we have the relation:

$$\varepsilon \leqslant 1 \Leftrightarrow E_C \leqslant 1 \tag{3.9}$$

Again, rearranging the elasticity of cost: $E_C = (dC/dq) \ / \ (C/q)$, we see that the elasticity of cost is the ratio of marginal cost $(dC/dq)$ to average cost $(C/q)$:
    Therefore

$$E_C = MC/AC \tag{3.10}$$

We know from the analysis in Chapter 2 that the MC curve intersects the AC curve at the latter's minimum point. If the AC curve has the normal U-shape, we know that MC is larger than AC for points beyond that and less than AC for output levels less than at $AC_{min}$. From this, and the relations (3.8) and (3.10) follows the following simple relation between average cost curves and the elasticity of scale:

| *Elasticity of scale* | *Average costs* |
|:---:|:---:|
| $> 1$ | Falling |
| $= 1$ | Constant |
| $< 1$ | Rising |

This relation is intuitively obvious: if $\varepsilon > 1$, we know that doubling of inputs (and thus a doubling of all costs) must lead to a more than doubling of output. Hence average cost must fall (and vice versa when $\varepsilon < 1$).

## 3.5   The Elasticity of Substitution

Apart from the scale effect there is also the substitution effect. The substitution effect is clearly determined by the shape of the isoquant. Very 'shallow' isoquants will have large sustitution effects whereas very sharply curved isoquants will have relatively small substitution effects. An elegant parameter for summarising the shape of an isoquant was devised by Hicks (1932) and is called the *elasticity of substitution.*

The elasticity of substitution is defined as the ratio of the proportionate change in factor proportions to the proportionate change in the slope of the isoquant.

Factor proportions are $v_1/v_2$ and the change in factor proportions is $d(v_1/v_2)$ hence the proportionate change in factor proportions is $d(v_1/v_2) / (v_1/v_2)$.

The slope of the isoquant is $(dv_1/dv_2)$ and the change in that slope is $d(dv_1/dv_2)$ hence the proportionate change of slope is

$$d\left(\frac{dv_1}{dv_2}\right) \bigg/ \left(\frac{dv_1}{dv_2}\right)$$

Putting all this together, we get that the elasticity of substitution ($\sigma$) is:

$$\sigma = \frac{\left[ d\left(\dfrac{v_1}{v_2}\right) \Big/ \left(\dfrac{v_1}{v_2}\right) \right]}{\left[ d\left(\dfrac{dv_1}{dv_2}\right) \Big/ \left(\dfrac{dv_1}{dv_2}\right) \right]} \tag{3.11}$$

This may look like a fairly complicated expression but as we shall see, it in fact turns out to be very simple when applied to many standard forms of production function.

One point to note here is that for cost minimisation the slope of the isoquant ($dv_1/dv_2$) is equal to relative factor prices—($P_2/P_1$). This means that if cost minimisation is assumed we can redefine the elasticity of substitution as the ratio of the proportionate change in factor proportions $[d(v_1/v_2)/(v_1/v_2)]$ to proportionate change in relative factor prices $[d(P_2/P_1)/(P_2/P_1)]$.

Thus for example if we know that the elasticity of substitution is 0.1 then we know that a 10 per cent change in relative factor prices will bring about a 1 per cent change in factor proportions ($0.1 \times 10$ per cent). If on the other hand the elasticity of substitution were 5.0 then a 10 per cent change in relative factor prices would bring about a 50 per cent change in factor proportions ($5.0 \times 10$ per cent).

Thus the elasticity of substitution is a very simple way of describing how technology would change in response to change in relative prices (e.g. the effect on employment of an oil price rise).

A third way of expressing the elasticity of substitution is in terms of the partial derivatives of the production function, that is

$$\sigma = -\frac{f_1 \cdot f_2}{v_1 \cdot v_2} \cdot \frac{(v_1 \cdot f_1 + v_2 \cdot f_2)}{(f_{11} \cdot f_2^2 - 2f_1 \cdot f_2 \cdot f_{12} + f_{22} \cdot f_1^2)} \tag{3.12}$$

where $f_i$ is the first order partial with respect to $v_1$, $f_{11}$ is the second order partial with respect to $v_1$ and $f_{12}$ is the cross partial.

The derivation of (3.12) is given in the appendix to this chapter.

We also have that for any function:

$$q = f(v_1, v_2)$$

$$\frac{q dq}{q} = f_1 v_1 \frac{dv_1}{v_1} + f_2 v_2 \frac{dv_2}{v_2}$$

and for *scale* changes we have that

$$\frac{dv_1}{v_1} = \frac{dv_2}{v_2} = \frac{dv}{v}$$

therefore

$$q\left(\frac{dq}{q} \bigg/ \frac{dv}{v}\right) = f_1 v_1 + f_2 v_2$$

but

$$\left(\frac{dq}{q} \bigg/ \frac{dv}{v}\right) = \varepsilon$$

therefore (3.12) becomes

$$\sigma = -\frac{f_1 f_2 \varepsilon q}{v_1 \cdot v_2 (f_{11} \cdot f_2^2 - 2f_1 \cdot f_2 \cdot f_{12} + f_{22} \cdot f_1^2)} \tag{3.13}$$

Furthermore, when there are constant returns to scale we have that:

$$f_{11} = -(v_2/v_1) \cdot f_{12} \qquad f_{22} = (v_1/v_2) \cdot f_{12}$$

Thus (3.13) becomes after simplification

$$\sigma = \frac{f_1 \cdot f_2 \cdot q}{f_{12}[v_2^2 \cdot f_2^2 + 2v_1 \cdot v_2 \cdot f_1 \cdot f_2 + v_1^2 \cdot f_1^2]}$$

Therefore

$$\sigma = \frac{f_1 \cdot f_2 \cdot q}{f_{12} \cdot [v_1 \cdot f_1 + v_2 \cdot f_2]^2}$$

but $v_1 \cdot f_1 + v_2 \cdot f_2 = q$, since $\varepsilon = 1$ and hence:

$$\sigma = \frac{f_1 \cdot f_2}{f_{12} \cdot q} \tag{3.14}$$

for constant returns to scale.

## 3.6    Factor Demand and Elasticity of Substitution

We can now say something about the isoquants shown in Figure 1.6. Isoquant (a) has a rectangular shape in which production will always occur at the corner. Hence no change in factor proportions will ever occur no matter what happens to relative factor prices. Thus the elasticity of substitution of isoquant (a) is zero.

Isoquant (b) is a straight line cutting both axes. In this case for all isocost lines with slopes greater than the isoquant only factor 2 will be used. For all isocost lines of slope less than the isoquant only factor 1 will be used. When the slope of the isocost equals the slope of the isoquant then any combination of factors may be used. Thus as relative factor prices are changed, they at first have no effect. Then, at the point when the two lines have the same slope any ratio can arise. Thereafter there will be a complete switch to the previously idle factor.

Thus the elasticity of substitution is infinity where it is not zero. These shaped isoquants are said to have infinite elasticity of substitution. Thus the elasticity of substitution ranges from zero (case (a)) to infinity (case (b)) and covers all points between. Isoquant (c) for example is an intermediate case in which the change in relative factor prices will precipitate some change in relative factor proportions but no sharp jumps as in isoquant (b).

If we define the elasticity of demand for a factor as:

$$E_j = -\left(\frac{dv_j}{v_j} \bigg/ \frac{dP_j}{P_j}\right) \tag{3.15}$$

it can be shown (see Allen, 1938, pp. 372–3) that the relationship between $E_j$ and $\sigma$ is of the form

$$E_j = S_j \sigma \tag{3.16}$$

where $S_j$ is the proportion of total cost which is due to the input $j$, that is

$$S_j = \frac{v_j P_j}{\sum\limits_{i=1}^{n} v_i P_i}$$

*This result holds only for constant returns to scale.*

Similarly we can define the *cross* price elasticity of demand for factors $i$ and $j$ as

$$E_{ji} \equiv -(dv_j/v_j)/dP_i/P_i \tag{3.17}$$

that is the cross-elasticity of demand is the proportionate change in the demand for one factor in response to a proportionate change in the price of another factor.

If $E_{ji} > 0$, then increasing the price of $i$ causes a reduction in the demand for $j$ and $i$ and $j$ are said to be *complements*.

If $E_{ji} < 0$, then $j$ and $i$ are said to be *substitutes*. In the two-factor case considered here the factors must be either substitutes or have a cross-elasticity of zero. It is not possible to maintain production and decrease the use of both inputs as would be implied by complementarity when a factor price increased.

When more than two factors are considered it is possible for complementarity to exist between two factors but at least two of the '$n$' factors must be substitutes.

It can be shown that the cross-price elasticity can be calculated from:

$$E_{21} = S_2 \cdot \sigma$$

where $S_2$ is factor 2's share in the cost.

*These results hold only for the two-factor fixed output case and the elasticity of substitution has been defined here only for the two input cases.*

The elasticity of substitution discussed so far deals only with the two-input case and hence its direction of movement (along the isoquant) is unambiguous. However, when there are three or more inputs the possibility of ambiguity is opened up. One rather straightforward answer is to define the elasticity of substitution between any two inputs *with all other inputs held constant*, that is a 'partial' elasticity of substitution. This specifies a two-input isoquant in an $n$ input world and hence removes any ambiguity. The elasticity between any two inputs may therefore depend on the values taken by the other (fixed) inputs.

The alternative to fixing the *quantities* of all other inputs is to fix the *prices* of all other inputs. This elasticity would be measured between the cost minimising combination of inputs before the price of a factor is changed and the cost minimising combination of factors after the price change.

Typically this would involve substituting some of each input for the input whose price changed.

It should be stressed that whether the elasticity of substitution is measured with $n-2$ inputs fixed or with $n-1$ prices fixed it is measured on *one* isoquant – output is fixed. These definitions are of course identical when there are only two inputs hence the absence of ambiguity in the two-input case.

The 'fixed price' version of this multi-input case is:

$$\sigma_{rs} = \left[ \frac{v_1 f_1 + v_2 f_2 \ldots v_n f_n}{v_r v_s} \right] \frac{F_{rs}}{|F|}$$

where $F_{rs}$ is the cofactor of $f_{rs}$ in $F$ which is the matrix of derivatives:

$$F = \begin{matrix} 0 & f_1 & f_2 & \cdots & f_n \\ f_1 & f_{11} & f_{12} & \cdots & f_{1n} \\ f_2 & f_{21} & f_{22} & \cdots & \vdots \\ \vdots & \vdots & \vdots & & \\ f_n & f_{n1} & & \cdots & f_{nn} \end{matrix}$$

(see appendix of this chapter).

## 3.7 Putty–Clay Technology

We have already drawn a distinction between the long-run (*ex ante*) choice set and the short-run (*ex post*) decision set. The difference turns on the inability to increase or decrease the cost of capital inputs in the short run. Thus, in the short run, only a subset of factors can be set at their optimum levels.

A second distinction is also possible. This is the assumption that *ex ante* there is the possibility of substituting capital for labour (the elasticity of substitution is not zero), but that *ex post* (once the capital is installed) it is no longer possible to substitute labour for capital. Thus, *ex post*, the elasticity of substitution is zero. *Ex ante* the entrepreneur can choose any point on any isoquant but *ex post* he is stuck with that point. Once the plant is installed he has not only a fixed amount of capital but will need a fixed amount of labour to operate it.

This is the so-called *putty–clay* technology: Putty *ex ante* and clay *ex* post.

Putty technology dominates most neoclassical models in which labour is assumed to be a variable input into an economy. Indeed, *ex-post* substitution is almost casually assumed in much current economic theory.

On the other hand, clay technology is assumed in the inter-industry or input–output approach to economic modelling. This is the approach of Leontief who focuses on the flows of intermediates between industries and explains the demand for these inputs (and for other factors) in terms of the output being produced rather than in terms of factor prices.

In a clay world the entrepreneur is constrained to operate with fixed factor proportions. His output decision will determine his factor inputs. This is shown in Figure 3.2. *Ex ante* he can choose a level of

**FIGURE 3.2**

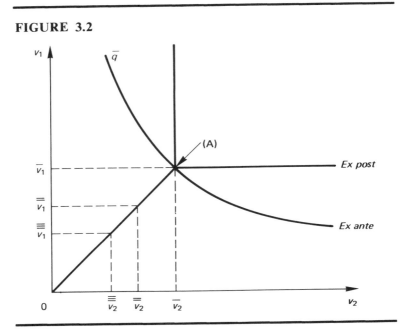

output and any factor combination on that isoquant. If he chooses point (A) on $\bar{q}$ then he is stuck thereafter with those particular factor proportions $(\bar{v}_2, \bar{v}_1)$. His isoquant is now rectangular. If he wishes to reduce output he must move back along ray 0A, say to $\bar{\bar{v}}_1, \bar{\bar{v}}_2$ or $\bar{\bar{\bar{v}}}_1, \bar{\bar{\bar{v}}}_2$.

The variation in $v_1$ and $v_2$ with output is also assumed to be linear, implying constant returns to scales. Thus, halving output will halve all inputs. The ratio of any particular input $v_1$ to the output $q_j$, $[v_i/q_j]$ is constant and is called the *input–output coefficient* as is usually denoted as $a_{ij}$: the amount of $i$ needed to produce one unit of $j$.

### 3.8 Putty–Clay and Frontier Production Functions

Although it is customary in production theory to consider either the *ex post* or the *ex ante* (SR versus LR) choice set and decision it is obvious that in the real world there will be a range of possibilities. Firms which invested long ago may have had rather different expectations about future factor prices than would those which invested comparatively recently. This means that there is no uniform 'clay'. Each piece of capital may have its own particular characteristics depending on the factor price ratio obtaining at the time of its manufacture.

It is also possible that the 'putty' too changed over time, that is the *ex ante* choice set changed with time. If the choice set were enlarged over time then it is called *technological progress*, implying that the same output can be produced with less input. If this improvement can only be had by investing in new capital, then it is confined to the *ex ante* choice set and the *ex post* points remain unchanged by the passage of time.

Thus there are two influences bearing on the 'clay' currently in existence. First as relative prices change the choice of clay will move around the isoquant so that later 'vintages' of capital will have more appropriate factor proportions. Second as technological progress occurs, younger vintages will be more 'productive'.

Both these points are illustrated in Figure 3.3. At time $t_0$ the *ex*-ante (putty) choice set is represented by isoquant ($t_0$) and the factor price ratio at $t_0$ yields isocost line $t_0$. This leads to the choice of factor combination (A) at time $t_0$. Hence all capital installed at time $t_0$ will require that particular factor ratio for its entire life.

Later, at time $t_1$, technological progress has occurred and moved the isoquant to $t_1$ (nearer the origin). During the same period $v_1$ has become relatively more expensive so that the isocost line $t_1$ has become less steeply sloped.

At time $t_1$, therefore, the choice of technology will be at B and all capital installed at time $t_1$ will require that amount of labour throughout its life.

The situation described above is referred to as the 'embodiment hypothesis'. This means that technological progress is embodied in the capital structure and that technological progress cannot be manifested in a firm without altering the concrete pieces of capital. Since capital equipment generally lasts for some years (in national accounts this is assumed to be twenty years on average), this also implies that each firm has to live with a technology which is not completely up to date.

The existence of embodied technological progress has led to the introduction of *frontier production functions*. The frontier production function is the function representing the best (i.e. the most

**FIGURE 3.3**
**Illustration of the Concept of Frontier Production Function**

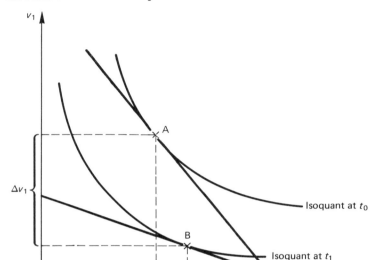

modern) technology. It is called a 'frontier' function because it represents the efficiency frontier of the industry, the best that can be done with all modern equipment. Frontier production functions are also called 'best practice' functions or '*ex-ante*' production functions. These functions are closely related to what we have called long-run production functions, since the firm can, in the long run, choose the best technology.

The introduction of frontier production functions has inspired the studies of *efficiency* in an industry. The measure of efficiency is derived by seeing how the technologies of individual firms within an industry compare with the industry's frontier function. The main features of this idea can easily be illustrated if we assume constant returns to scale and study the *unit isoquant*. Consider Figure 3.4.

Let AA denote the isoquant of the frontier production function for output level = 1. (The points on this isoquant are accordingly the

**FIGURE 3.4**
**Illustration of the Measure of Efficiency**

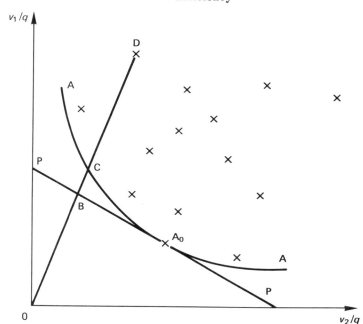

imput coefficients of the best technology currently available.) The crosses denote observable input coefficients for the firms in the industry. (*Note.* Each cross is a *per unit of output* coefficient.) The line PP is the current isocost line (minimum cost of producing one unit of output) and the point $A_0$ is accordingly the best technology given today's factor prices and today's isoquant.

Let $D$ be a specific firm. If we could have chosen the best technology, *but kept the factor proportions of D*, we would have chosen the technology represented by C. Comparing the amount of factors at C and D can obviously form a basis for efficiency comparisons. Following the definitions given by Farrell (1957), we define *the technical efficiency of D* (TE) as

$$TE = OC/OD \qquad (3.18)$$

TE equals 1 if the firm can choose technology from AA. It approaches zero as the distance between C and D grows. Thus technical efficiency has the range $0 \to 1$.

However, even point C is not the most profitable technology. It is technically efficient, but it does not represent the most profitable factor combination given the existing factor prices. Hence the firm D has also a *'price-inefficiency'* caused by non-optimal factor proportions. Farrell defines the *price-efficiency* of D(PE) as:

$$PE = OB/OC \qquad (3.19)$$

This is the ratio of: the cost of producing with best technology (i.e. on AA) but with D's factor proportions; and the cost of producing with best technology *and* with best factor proportions. It is accordingly a measure of the excess cost resulting from inappropriate factor proportions.

It is possible to combine the technical and the price efficiency measures to an overall measure of the efficiency of *D*. Again, following Farrell, we define the *economic efficiency* of *D* (EE) as:

$$EE = TE \cdot PE = OB/OD \qquad (3.20)$$

The measure of economic efficiency equals the ratio between unit production cost with the best technology (at $A_0$) and the unit production cost of firm *D* at current factor prices.

These efficiency measures may be generated for each firm in the industry. By adding all numbers (weighted by the firm's share of the total industry's output) we can also obtain measures of the efficiency of the whole industry. These measures are called *structural efficiency measures*.

Thus, for example, if there were three firms in the industry with efficiencies 1, 0.5 and 0.3 respectively and firm 1 were half the size of firm 2 which was half the size of firm 3, we would have measure of structural efficiency of

$$1 \times \tfrac{4}{7} + 0.5 \times \tfrac{2}{7} + 0.3 \times \tfrac{1}{7} = 0.757 = 75.7\%$$

It is important to note that there need not be any avoidable inefficiency involved. There may well be a difference between the technology of an existing firm and the best practice technology. But it may be perfectly rational for firm D to stay where it is since scrapping of all its existing equipment and moving to the point $A_0$ would (compared with the present situation) cause heavy losses. Our efficiency measures are essentially only a comparison between the existing and the best technology. They tell us something about the extent of 'vintage' capital and of the posssibilities of improvement, but they do not indicate that firms behave irrationally, nor that we should move to best practice technology 'at any cost'.

## 3.9 Long- and Short-run Industrial Supply Curves

This idea of a frontier production function and its distinction between an *ex ante* production function and an *ex post* industrial structure, may be used to clarify the relationship between the long- and short-run industry supply curves. We could define a long-run supply curve by stipulating that all firms should incorporate the best technology (including the best factor proportions) and that all firms should be built to optimal scale, that is the scale giving the lowest possible unit cost. This is a natural definition: when we speak of the long run we mean that all kinds of adjustments have taken place. There is no room for firms with a non-optimal technology or a non-optimal scale since such firms would have been driven out of market by the competition.

Accordingly, we can speak of a long-run supply curve which is horizontal and equal to $ATC_{min}$ of the frontier production function. Any market price higher than $ATC_{min}$ will lead to the establishment of new firms which see the opportunity of making profits. Their entry will cause market price to fall. Any market price below $ATC_{min}$ will lead to the closing down of some firms (since they are making losses) (and hence an increase in price).

The *short-run industry supply curve* is derived from the existing technological structure in which only *variable* costs matter.

We assume now, in line with the 'clay' nature of capital, that the firm's technology can be characterised by a list of *constant input coefficients* – one coefficient for each of the variable factors. If labour is the only variable factor this means that we assume that a firm uses, say, $X$ units of labour per unit of output irrespective of the total amount of production up to some *capacity ceiling*.

Our assumptions imply that each firm has a constant variable unit cost. If the firms are denoted by $i$ $(i = 1, 2, \ldots, N)$, we call this unit variable cost $AVC^i$. Since $AVC^i$ is constant up to capacity ceiling, it is also equal to the marginal cost of the firm: $AVC^i = MC^i$. We can now obtain a very simple rule for the short-run industry supply curve. If market price exceeds unit variable cost for a firm $i$, then that firm can cover its variable cost and hence will produce at full capacity. If, on the other hand, market price is below $AVC^i$, the firms will stop operation and close since its average variable (avoidable) costs exceed revenue. Consider now Figure 3.5. In this figure we have ordered the firms according to the variable unit cost to obtain an increasing step function. The length of each step equals the capacity of the firm, and the height of each step equals the difference between the firm's AVC and the AVC of the next best firm. *This is the short-run industry supply curve.* If, for instance, market demand equals the line denoted DD, we see that firms $1, \ldots, 4$ will all be operating at full capacity (since $P > AVC$) but that firm 5 and 6 will be closed down. The market price will be $P^x$ and quantity sold $Q^x$. If the demand curve moved to the left, then more firms would close and hence supply would fall.

In Figure 3.5 we have also indicated the long-run price – MIN AVERAGE *TOTAL* COST – ($ATC_{min}$). The long-run supply curve is a horizontal line from that point. The long-run price is in our case below the existing price. This means that it will be profitable to build new firms with best practice technology since minimum total unit costs are lower than current market price. These new firms will increase supply and force the price down to the long-run equilibrium level (i.e. until $P = ATC_{min}$). If, on the other hand, the long run average total cost curve is located above the existing price, new firms will not be profitable (even best practice firms). In that case the price will remain at $P^x$ until the oldest units have become obsolete and the long-run supply curve has shifted downwards. New plants will not be built until the long-run supply curve has fallen below the existing price. We thus have the rule that *the unit variable cost of the least efficient plant must exceed the unit total cost of a new plant if a new plant is to be built.*

## Appendix

### *The elasticity of substitution in the general n-factor case*

The elasticity is defined above only for the two-factor case. It is also obvious that we cannot immediately extend our definition to the general $n$-factor case since we cannot speak unambiguously of 'factor proportions' and 'slope' when more than two factors are involved.

**FIGURE 3.5**
**Illustration of the Short-run Supply Curve**

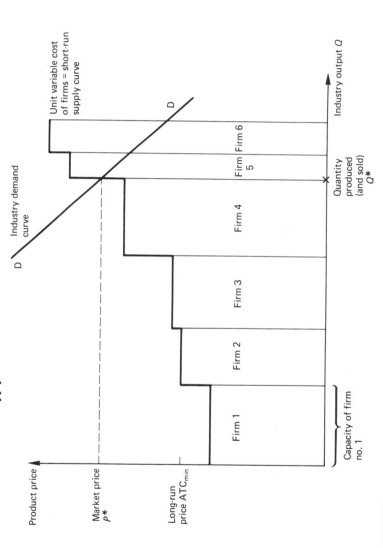

R. G. D. Allen (1938) has developed measures that can be used in the general case. We call these *Allen partial elasticities of substitution*, in short, AES.

Assume we have a production function:

$$q = f(v_1, \ldots, v_n) \tag{A3.1}$$

Define $F$ as the determinant of the bordered Hessian to $f(\ )$, that is as

$$
F = 
\begin{matrix}
0 & f_1 & f_2, & \cdots & f_n \\
f_1 & f_{11} & f_{12} & \cdots & f_{1n} \\
f_2 & & & & \\
\vdots & & & & \\
f_n & f_{n1} & & \cdots & f_{nn}
\end{matrix}
\tag{A3.2}
$$

where $f_i$ denotes the first-order $f_{ij}$ the second-order partial derivatives of $f$. Now define $F_{rs}$ as the cofactor of $f_{rs}$ in $F$. Then we define the AES between factor $r$ and factor $s$ as:

$$\sigma_{rs} = (v_1 f_1 + v_2 f_2 + \cdots + v_n f_n)/(v_r v_s) \cdot (F_{rs}/F) \tag{A3.3}$$

This definition applies also to the two-factor case. Observe also that $\sigma_{rs} = \sigma_{sr}$ for all $s, r$.

## The relation between the elasticity of substitution and the price elasticities in the general case

The firm adjusts its demand for factors of production according to the factor prices. Accordingly we can define various price elasticities for the firm's demand for inputs. We define the elasticity of demand for factor $s$ with respect to changes in the price of factor $r$; $P_{rs}$, as:

$$P_{rs} = (dv_s/dP_r) \cdot (P_r/v_s) \tag{A3.4}$$

These price elasticities are of course most important when we wish to forecast the effects of a price-change. The relation between the AES and the price elasticities (we assume output to be constant) are:

$$P_{rs} = S_r \cdot \sigma_{rs} \tag{A3.5}$$

where $S_r$ is the cost-share factor $v_r = (v_r P_r / \Sigma_i v_i P_i)$. Thus, our price elasticities can easily be calculated once we know our AES. Observe that although $\sigma_{rs} = \sigma_{sr}$, we have in general $P_{rs} \neq P_{sr}$ because in general $S_r \neq S_s$.

If $P_{rs} < 0$, then the factors are said to be *complements*, if $P_{rs} > 0$, they are *substitutes*. It is always true that $P_{rr} < 0$.

## The elasticity of substitution and the cost functions

Assume that we have the following cost function associated with our production function:

$$C = H(q, P_1, \ldots, P_n) \tag{A3.6}$$

If $q = 1$, then we obtain the unit cost function $C = G(P_1, \ldots, P_n)$ Uzawa has shown that the AES can be calculated from this function by the formula:

$$\sigma_{rs} = (G \cdot G_{ij})/(G_i \cdot G_j) \tag{A3.7}$$

where $G_i$ denotes the first-order and $G_{ij}$ the second-order partial derivative of $G$ (or $H$) with respect to factor prices.

## Expressing the elasticity of substitution in terms of the partial derivatives of the production function

We have

$$\sigma = \frac{\mathrm{d}(v_1/v_2)}{(v_1/v_2)} \frac{(\mathrm{d}v_1/\mathrm{d}v_2)}{\mathrm{d}(\mathrm{d}v_1/\mathrm{d}v_2)} \tag{A3.8}$$

and $\sigma$ is defined along an isoquant so that $v_1$ and $v_2$ are constrained by:

$$\bar{q} = f(v_1, v_2) \tag{A3.9}$$

where $\bar{q}$ is the chosen level of output.

We next split (A3.8) into four parts and derive expressions for each part in turn before bringing them back into (A3.8). The four parts are: (a) $\mathrm{d}v_1/\mathrm{d}v_2$, (b) $\mathrm{d}(\mathrm{d}v_1/\mathrm{d}v_2)$, (c) $\mathrm{d}(v_1/v_2)$, and (d) $v_1/v_2$ and we take them in that order.

From (A3.9) we have $0 = f_1 \,\mathrm{d}v_1 + f_2 \,\mathrm{d}v_1$, that is

$$\frac{\mathrm{d}v_1}{\mathrm{d}v_2} = -\frac{f_2}{f_1} \tag{A3.10}$$

We also have:

$$d(dv_1/dv_2) = -d(f_2/f_1)$$

$$= -\left[\frac{f_{22}}{f_1} - \frac{f_2 f_{12}}{f_1^2}\right]dv_2 + \left[\frac{f_{21}}{f_1} - \frac{f_2 f_{11}}{f_1^2}\right]dv_1$$

$$= dv_2\left[\left\{\frac{f_{22}}{f_1} - \frac{f_2 f_{12}}{f_1^2}\right\} + \frac{dv_1}{dv_2}\left\{\frac{f_{21}}{f_1} - \frac{f_2 f_{11}}{f_1^2}\right\}\right]$$

but, from (A3.10)

$$\frac{dv_1}{dv_2} = -\frac{f_2}{f_1}$$

$$\therefore \ d(dv_1/dv_2) = -dv_2\left[\frac{f_{22}}{f_1} - \frac{f_2 f_{12}}{f_1^2} - \frac{f_{21}}{f_1^2}f_2 + \frac{f_2^2}{f_1^3}f_{11}\right]$$

$$d(dv_1/dv_2) = -\frac{dv_2}{f_1^3}[f_{22}f_1^2 - 2f_2 f_1 f_{12} + f_2^2 f_{11}] \tag{A3.11}$$

Finally

$$d(v_1/v_2) = \frac{dv_1}{v_2} - \frac{v_1 dv_2}{v_2^2} = \frac{dv_2}{v_2}\left[\frac{dv_1}{dv_2} - \frac{v_1}{v_2}\right]$$

$$d(v_1/v_2) = \frac{dv_2}{v_2^2 f_1}[v_1 f_1 + v_2 f_2] \tag{A3.12}$$

Putting (A3.10), (A3.11) and (A3.12) into (A3.8) we get

$$\sigma = \frac{f_1 f_2(v_1 f_1 + v_2 f_2)}{v_1 v_2(f_{22}f_1^2 - 2f_2 f_1 f_{12} + f_2^2 f_{11})} \tag{3.13}$$

## Selected Reading

Early derivations of the elasticity of scale can be found in W. E. Johnson, 'The Pure Theory of Utility Curves' (1913), *Economic Journal*, XXII, p. 507; E. Schneider, *Theorie der Produktion* (1934) p. 10 and S. Carlsson, *A Study on the Pure Theory of Production* (1939), p. 17 ff. Early definitions of the elasticity of cost are found in E. Schneider, 'Theorie der Produktion', pp. 34–5 and S. Carlsson, *A Study on the Pure Theory of Production*, pp. 43–4.

The elasticity of substitution was devised in J. R. Hicks, *The Theory of Wages* (1932), pp. 242–6. Partial elasticities, and the relation between the price and substitution elasticities are calculated in R. G. D. Allen, *Mathematical Analysis for Economists* (1938), p. 503 ff. For a more general survey of the relation between the diffferent elasticities see T. Puu, 'Les Effets de Substitution et D'Expansion dans le Theorie de la Production' (1966), *Revue D'Economie Politique*, LXXVI, pp. 57–91, summarised and condensed in T. Puu, 'Complementarity, Substitutivity and Regressivity in the Theory of Production' (1968), in *Recherches recentes sur la Fonction de Production*.

The putty–clay production model was first analysed by L. Johansen: 'Substitution versus Fixed Production Coefficients in the Theory of Economic Growth' (1959), *Econometrica*, XXVII, pp. 157–76 and by W. E. G. Salter in *Productivity and Technical Change* (1960). For an example of an empirical vintage model see Malcomson and Prior (1972).

Frontier production functions was first noted by A. P. Grosse in 'The Technological Structure of the Cotton Textile Industry' (1953), in W. Leontief (ed.) *Studies in the Structure of the American Economy*. The article by D. J. Aigner and S. F. Chu, 'On Estimating the Industry Production Function' (1968), *The American Economic Review*, 58 (4) 226–39 caused a renewed interest in the empirical estimations of frontier functions.

The theory of measuring the efficiency of firms and industry was introduced by M. J. Farrell in 'The Measurement of Productive Efficiency' (1957), *Journal of the Royal Statistical Society*, Series A (General), Part III, 129, pp. 253–90 and extended in M. J. Farrell and M. Fieldhouse: 'Estimating Efficient Production Functions under Increasing Returns to Scale' (1962), *Journal of the Royal Statistical Society*, Series A (General), 125, 252–67.

# The Cobb–Douglas Function

# 4

## 4.1  Introduction

Without doubt the most widely known production function is the Cobb–Douglas function. It owes part of its name to Professor Paul Douglas who, from empirical observations, inferred its properties, and part to his colleague Cobb, a mathematician, who suggested the mathematical form. Douglas had drawn a graph of the capital stock, total labour force and GNP for the US manufacturing industries for the period 1899–1922. He discovered that the difference between the log of capital and the log of GNP was always about three times greater than the difference between the log of the labour force and the log of GNP. It was this constant which caused Cobb to suggest the form

$$q = A v_1^{\alpha} v_2^{1-\alpha} \tag{4.1}$$

where $q$ is valued added, $v_1$ is capital stock and $v_2$ is employment. All for US manufacturing.

This function (4.1) had earlier been used by Wicksell but it was undoubtedly Douglas who secured it its popularity.

For reasons which will be made clear below, Cobb and Douglas constrained the exponents of $v_1$ and $v_2$ to sum to unity. But it is an unnecessary restriction and (4.1) may be generalised to

$$q = A v_1^{\alpha} v_2^{\beta} \tag{4.2}$$

A further generalisation would be to recognise the possibility of there being many inputs. Thus (4.2) becomes

$$q = A v_1^\alpha v_2^\beta v_3^\theta v_4^\lambda \ldots v_n^\Omega$$

## 4.2 Cobb–Douglas Isoquants

The equation for an isoquant is obtained if we fix the value of output, $\bar{q} = q$. We then obtain:

$$\bar{q} = A v_1^\alpha v_2^\beta \qquad dq = \alpha A v_1^{\alpha-1} v_2^\beta dv_1 + \beta A v_1^\alpha v_2^{\beta-1} dv_2 \tag{4.3}$$

Rearranging, we find:
$\text{Let } dq = 0, \ \dfrac{dv_2}{dv_1} = -\dfrac{\alpha q}{v_1} \Big/ \dfrac{\beta q}{v_2} = -\dfrac{\alpha}{\beta} \dfrac{v_2}{v_1}$

$$v_2 = (\bar{q}/A)^{1/\beta} v_1^{-\alpha/\beta} \tag{4.4}$$

which can be used as the equation for the isoquant for $q = \bar{q}$. We observe from (4.4) that the isoquants never touch the axes. When $v_1$ approaches infinity, $v_2$ approaches, but never equals, zero. The same is true for $v_1$ when $v_2$ approaches infinity. Thus all isoquants of the Cobb–Douglas function are asymptotic to the axes no matter what level of output is chosen. Furthermore, since neither input can go to zero, it is necessary in a Cobb–Douglas world to have some of both inputs: it is not possible to produce anything at all unless all the inputs are available.

The slope of the isoquant can be obtained by differentiating (4.4).

$$\frac{dv_2}{dv_1} = -\left(\frac{\alpha}{\beta}\right)\left(\frac{\bar{q}}{A}\right)^{-1/\beta} v_1^{-(1+\alpha/\beta)} \tag{4.5}$$

but

$$\left(\frac{\bar{q}}{A}\right)^{1/\beta} v_1^{-\alpha/\beta} = v_2 \qquad \text{(from (4.4))}$$

hence:

$$\frac{dv_2}{dv_1} = -\left(\frac{\alpha}{\beta}\right)\left(\frac{v_2}{v_1}\right) \tag{4.6}$$

Thus the isoquant always slopes downwards and is proportional to the factor proportions $(v_2/v_1)$ *irrespective of the level of output.* Thus, the isoquant slope is the same along each factor ray through the origin (i.e. any $v_2/v_1$) and we conclude that the Cobb–Douglas production function is *homothetic.*

A typical isoquant is shown in Figure 4.1.

**FIGURE 4.1**

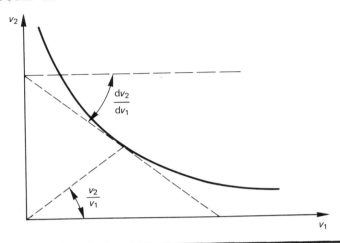

## 4.3 Short-run Total, Average and Marginal Product Curves for Cobb–Douglas

By short run is meant that time period during which one of the two inputs is deemed to be fixed. Thus, for example, fixing $v_1$ at $\bar{v}_1$ yields:

$$q = A \cdot \bar{v}_1^\alpha \cdot v_2^\beta \tag{4.7}$$

or

$$q = B \cdot v_2^\beta$$

where $B$ is $A\bar{v}_1^\alpha$ = constant by assumption.

The SR total product curve can be derived directly from (4.7) which relates output ($q$) to the quantity of $v_2$. (4.7) implies that if $0 < \beta < 1$, then $q$ will always increase with $v_2$ but will do so at an ever decreasing rate. This may be more clearly seen from the SR average product curve. Let the SR average product of $v_2$ be $APv_2$ then:

$$APv_2 = \frac{q}{v_2} = Bv_2^{\beta-1} \tag{4.8}$$

From (4.8) it is clear that if $\beta < 1$ $APv_2$ always decreases as $v_2$

increases. Thus the 'productivity' of $v_2$ is a decreasing function of the quantity used. That is, the marginal product of $v_2$ is a decreasing function of the quantity used. (the law of diminishing returns).

The marginal product of $v_2$ can be found by differentiating (4.7). Thus:

$$\text{MP}v_2 = \frac{dq}{dv^2} = \beta B v_2^{\beta-1} \tag{4.9}$$

In order for this to be positive $\beta > 0$ and in order for it to obey the law of diminishing returns $\beta < 1$. If $\beta$ is so constrained, then both the average and the marginal product curves slope downward. This is illustrated in Figure 4.2 where $A = 1.0$ and $v_1 = 10$.

---

**FIGURE 4.2**
**TP, AP and MP Curves of a C–D Production Function**

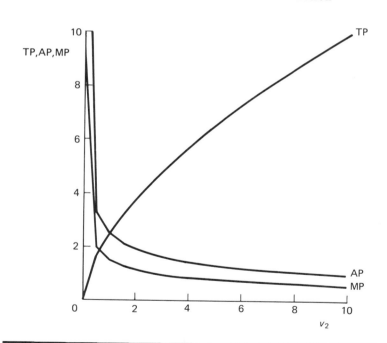

## 4.4   The Cobb–Douglas Elasticity of Substitution

The equation for the elasticity of substitution (given in Chapter 3) is:

$$\sigma = \frac{\mathrm{d}(v_2/v_1)}{(v_2/v_1)} \bigg/ \frac{\mathrm{d}(\mathrm{d}v_2/\mathrm{d}v_1)}{(\mathrm{d}v_2/\mathrm{d}v_1)} \qquad (4.10)$$

This is defined for a constant level of output thus

$$\bar{q} = Av_1^{\alpha} v_2^{\beta}$$

differentiating yields:

$$0 = A\alpha v_1^{\alpha-1} v_2^{\beta} \, \mathrm{d}v_1 + A\beta v_1^{\alpha} v_2^{\beta-1} \, \mathrm{d}v_2$$

Rearranging yields

$$\frac{\mathrm{d}v_2}{\mathrm{d}v_1} = -\frac{\alpha}{\beta}\left(\frac{v_2}{v_1}\right) \qquad (4.11a)$$

Differentiating the LHS w.r.t. $(v_2/v_1)$ yields

$$\mathrm{d}(\mathrm{d}v_2/\mathrm{d}v_1)/\mathrm{d}(v_2/v_1) = \frac{-\alpha}{\beta} \qquad (4.11b)$$

Rewriting (4.10) as:

$$\sigma = \frac{\mathrm{d}v_2/\mathrm{d}v_1}{v_2/v_1} \cdot \left(\frac{\mathrm{d}(\mathrm{d}v_2/\mathrm{d}v_1)}{\mathrm{d}(v_2/v_1)}\right)^{-1}$$

and substituting the results we obtained from (4.11a) and (4.11b) yields:

$$\sigma = \left(-\frac{\alpha}{\beta}\right) \cdot \left(-\frac{\alpha}{\beta}\right)^{-1} \qquad (4.12)$$

$$\sigma = 1.$$

Thus for the Cobb–Douglas function the elasticity of substitution is everywhere (for all levels of output and for any factor combination) equal to unity.

*Note:* If the first order conditions for the cost minimisation are satisfied, then

$$\left(\frac{\mathrm{d}v_2}{\mathrm{d}v_1}\right) = -\left(\frac{P_1}{P_2}\right) \quad \text{and} \quad \mathrm{d}\left(\frac{\mathrm{d}v_2}{\mathrm{d}v_1}\right) = -\mathrm{d}\left(\frac{P_1}{P_2}\right)$$

and (4.10) becomes

$$\sigma = \frac{d(v_2/v_1)}{(v_2/v_1)} \Big/ \frac{d(P_1/P_2)}{(P_1/P_2)} = 1$$

Hence for Cobb–Douglas functions a 10 per cent change in the factor price ratio leads to a 10 per cent change in the factor input ratio in the opposite direction, that is a 10 per cent increase in $P_1$ relative to $P_2$ will lead to a 10 per cent reduction in $v_1$ relative to $v_2$.

## 4.5 Returns to Scale and the Cobb–Douglas

From Chapter 3 we have for a two-input function:

$$\varepsilon = f_1\left(\frac{v_1}{q}\right) + f_2\left(\frac{v_2}{q}\right) \tag{4.13}$$

where $\varepsilon$ is the elasticity of scale and $f_i$ is $\partial q/\partial v_i$.

For the Cobb–Douglas case:

$$q = A v_1^\alpha v_2^\beta$$

and

$$\left.\begin{array}{l}
\dfrac{\partial q}{\partial v_1} = \alpha A v_1^{\alpha-1} v_2^\beta = \dfrac{\alpha q}{v_1} \\[3mm]
\dfrac{\partial q}{\partial v_2} = \beta A v_1^\alpha v_2^{\beta-1} = \dfrac{\beta q}{v_2}
\end{array}\right\} \tag{4.14}$$

Substituting (4.14) into (4.13) yields:

$$\varepsilon = \frac{\alpha q}{v_1}\left(\frac{v_1}{q}\right) + \frac{\beta q}{v^2}\left(\frac{v_2}{q}\right)$$

that is

$$\varepsilon = \alpha + \beta \tag{4.15}$$

Thus the elasticity of scale of the Cobb–Douglas function depends solely upon $\alpha$ and $\beta$. When $\alpha + \beta < 1$ there are decreasing returns to scale; when $\alpha + \beta = 1$ there are constant returns to scale; when $\alpha + \beta > 1$ there are increasing returns to scale.

Since $\alpha$ and $\beta$ are constants the elasticity of scale of the Cobb–Douglas function is also constant (that is to say it remains unchanged with output and/or factor proportions). This rules out the possibility of 'U'-shaped long-run cost curves unless input prices changes as factor demands grow. In perfectly competitive markets then an $\varepsilon > 1$ implies a falling average cost curve with no minimum point.

Conversely, if $\varepsilon < 1$ the long-run average cost curve steadily rises and minimum cost occurs as close to the origin as possible. Finally, if $\varepsilon = 1$ the long-run average cost curve is horizontal – scale has no effect on costs at all (cf. appendix to Chapter 2).

## 4.6   Cobb–Douglas Factor Demand Functions

The demand for inputs will clearly depend on the optimum scale of output and the optimum combination of inputs. For any given level of output the optimum combination of inputs is given by the cost minimising condition $(P_1/P_2 = \mathrm{d}v_2/\mathrm{d}v_1)$ and from equation (4.6) given above:

$$\frac{P_1}{P_2} = \frac{\mathrm{d}v_2}{\mathrm{d}v_1} = \left(\frac{\alpha}{\beta}\right)\left(\frac{v_2}{v_1}\right) \tag{4.16}$$

From (4.16)

$$v_1 = \left(\frac{\alpha}{\beta}\right)\left(\frac{P_2}{P_1}\right)v_2$$

and $\hspace{10cm}$ (4.17)

$$v_2 = \left(\frac{\beta}{\alpha}\right)\left(\frac{P_1}{P_2}\right)v_1$$

The production function is:

$$q = A v_1^\alpha v_2^\beta \tag{4.2}$$

Substituting (4.17) into (4.2) yields

$$q = A\left(\frac{\alpha}{\beta}\frac{P_2}{P_1}v_2\right)^\alpha v_2^\beta$$

and

$$q = A v_1^\alpha \left(\frac{\beta}{\alpha}\frac{P_1}{P_2}v_1\right)^\beta$$

From which:

$$v_1 = \left[\frac{q}{A}\left(\frac{P_2}{P_1}\frac{\alpha}{\beta}\right)^\beta\right]^{1/(\alpha+\beta)}$$

$$v_2 = \left[\frac{q}{A}\left(\frac{P_1}{P_2}\frac{\beta}{\alpha}\right)^\alpha\right]^{1/(\alpha+\beta)}$$

(4.18)

Equations (4.18) are factor demand equations and express the demand for the factors in terms of output and relative factor prices. They were derived from the Cobb–Douglas production function, with cost minimisation and perfectly competitive markets.

From (4.18)

$$\frac{dv_1}{dq} = \left[\frac{1}{A}\left(\frac{P_2}{P_1}\frac{\alpha}{\beta}\right)^\beta\right]^{1/(\alpha+\beta)}\frac{1}{(\alpha+\beta)}q^{1/(\alpha+\beta)-1}$$

Therefore

$$\frac{dv_1}{dq} = \frac{v_1}{q}\frac{1}{(\alpha+\beta)} \Rightarrow \underline{\frac{dv_1}{v_1}\bigg/\frac{dq}{q} = \frac{1}{(\alpha+\beta)}}$$

and similarly

$$\frac{dv_2}{dq} = \frac{v_2}{q}\frac{1}{(\alpha+\beta)} \Rightarrow \underline{\frac{dv_2}{v_2}\bigg/\frac{dq}{q} = \frac{1}{(\alpha+\beta)}}$$

Thus the elasticity of each factor input with respect to output $[dv_i/v_i)/(dq/q)]$ is the same and equals $1/(\alpha+\beta)$, from which it is clear that for constant returns to scale $(\alpha+\beta=1)$ the proportionate change in each factor $(dv_1/v_1)$ and $(dv_2/v_2)$, exactly equal proportionate change in output $(dq/q)$ that is the elasticity of input with respect to output is unity. Furthermore, the elasticity of demand for inputs with respect to relative input prices can be derived thus:

$$\frac{dv_1}{d(P_2/P_1)} = \left[\frac{1}{A}\left(\frac{\alpha}{\beta}\right)^\beta\right]^{1/(\alpha+\beta)}\frac{\beta}{(\alpha+\beta)}\left(\frac{P_2}{P_1}\right)^{\beta/(\alpha+\beta)-1}$$

$$= v_1\frac{\beta}{\alpha+\beta}\left(\frac{P_2}{P_1}\right)^{-1}$$

Therefore

$$\frac{dv_1}{v_1}\bigg/\frac{d(P_2/P_1)}{(P_2/P_1)} = \left(\frac{\beta}{\alpha+\beta}\right)$$

and similarly

$$\frac{dv_2}{v_2} \Big/ \frac{d(P_1/P_2)}{(P_1/P_2)} = \left(\frac{\alpha}{(\alpha+\beta)}\right)$$

Again it is clear that for constant returns to scale the elasticity of demand for $v_1$ with respect to $(P_1/P_2)$ is $\beta$ and the elasticity of demand for $v_2$ with respect to $(P_2/P_1)$ is $\alpha$.

### 4.7 Cobb–Douglas Cost Functions

Very often it is convenient to work in terms of cost and factor prices rather than output and factor inputs. The relationship between cost and factor prices is called a cost function and is a 'dual' of the underlying production function.

Total cost of production is defined as:

$$C = P_1 v_1 + P_2 v_2$$

But, from (4.18):

$$v_1 = \left[\frac{q}{A}\left(\frac{P_2}{P_1}\frac{\alpha}{\beta}\right)^\beta\right]^{1/\alpha+\beta}$$

and

$$v_2 = \left[\frac{q}{A}\left(\frac{P_1}{P_2}\frac{\beta}{\alpha}\right)^\alpha\right]^{1/\alpha+\beta}$$

Substituting these into the cost equation yields, after simplifications:

$$C = \left(\frac{q}{A}\right)^{1/\varepsilon} P_1^{\alpha/\varepsilon} P_2^{\beta/\varepsilon} \left(\frac{\alpha}{\beta}\right)^{\beta/\varepsilon} \left(\frac{\varepsilon}{\alpha}\right) \qquad (4.19)$$

where $\varepsilon$ = the elasticity of scale and = $\alpha+\beta$.

Equation (4.19) is the cost function of the Cobb–Douglas production function and clearly has the same algebraic form as the Cobb–Douglas function except that the exponents of $P_1$ and $P_2$ now sum to unity no matter what the values of $\alpha$ and $\beta$ are in the original function.

We have already shown that for the Cobb–Douglas function the returns to scale are the sum of the exponents.

Thus the elasticity of cost with respect to $P_1$ and $P_2$ is the sum of the exponents on $P_1$ and $P_2$. This means that doubling prices will always exactly double cost. Thus the $C - D$ cost function is always homogeneous of degree 1 in prices.

When the production function is itself constrained to have CRTS (4.19) simplifies to look even more like its parent Cobb–Douglas, thus:

$$C = \frac{q}{A} \left( \frac{P_1}{\alpha} \right)^{\alpha} \left( \frac{P_2}{\beta} \right)^{\beta}$$

Notice that from (4.19)

$$\frac{\partial C}{\partial P_1} = \left( \frac{q}{A} \right)^{1/\varepsilon} \frac{\alpha}{\varepsilon} P_1^{(\alpha/\varepsilon)-1} P_2^{\beta/\varepsilon} \left( \frac{\alpha}{\beta} \right)^{\beta/\varepsilon} \frac{\varepsilon}{\alpha}$$

but $(\alpha/\varepsilon) - 1 = -(\beta/\varepsilon)$ hence

$$\frac{\partial C}{\partial P_1} = \left[ \frac{q}{A} \left( \frac{\alpha P_2}{\beta P_1} \right)^{\beta} \right]^{1/\varepsilon}$$

which is exactly the same as equations (4.18) which are factor demand equations. Thus the Shephard lemma works for the Cobb–Douglas function. This is

$$\frac{\partial C}{\partial P_i} = \hat{v}_i$$

where $\hat{v}_i$ is the cost minimising level of input $i$.

The average cost function is easily derived from the total cost function (4.19)

$$\text{Average Cost} = \frac{C}{q} = A^{-(1/\varepsilon)} q^{(1/\varepsilon)-1} P_1^{\alpha/\varepsilon} P_2^{\beta/\varepsilon} \left( \frac{\alpha}{\beta} \right)^{\beta/\varepsilon} \left( \frac{\varepsilon}{\alpha} \right) \quad (4.20)$$

From (4.20) it is clear that average cost will increase with output ($q$) when there are decreasing returns to scale ($\varepsilon > 1$). They will decrease with output when $\varepsilon > 1$ and remain constant when $\varepsilon = 1$. For this last case (CRTS) (4.20) becomes:

$$\frac{C}{q} = (\alpha A)^{-1} P_1^{\alpha} P_2^{\beta} \left( \frac{\alpha}{\beta} \right)^{\beta}$$

The marginal cost function can be derived by differentiating the total cost function with respect to $q$. Thus:

$$\text{MC} = \frac{\partial C}{\partial q} = \frac{1}{\varepsilon} q^{(1/\varepsilon)-1} A^{1/\varepsilon} P_1^{\alpha/\beta} P_2^{\beta/\varepsilon} \left( \frac{\alpha}{\beta} \right)^{\beta/\varepsilon} \left( \frac{\varepsilon}{\alpha} \right) \quad (4.21)$$

Once again the shape depends only upon the elasticity of scale ($\varepsilon$).

When $\varepsilon < 1$, $\partial C/\partial q$ increases with $q$, when $\varepsilon = 1$, $\partial C/\partial q$ remains constant with $q$, and when $\varepsilon > 1$, $\partial C/\partial q$ decreases with $q$.

## 4.8  The Adding-up Problem

The Cobb–Douglas function was born out of an investigation into the shares of national income going to labour and capital respectively. The predictions of Cobb–Douglas are that, with perfectly competitive markets there will be no change in the distribution of income between capital and labour no matter what happens to their relative prices. If capital pushes its price up by 10 per cent relative to that of labour, then it will induce a 10 per cent reduction in the quantity of capital relative to labour. Thus the factor shares remain the same. This result is not, however, without its problems, one of which is rooted in the conflicting assumptions about the returns to scale of the function.

Consider the profit equation:

$$\pi = P \cdot q - P_1 v_1 - P_2 v_2$$

where $P$ is the product price and

$$q = A v_1^\alpha v_2^\beta$$

Hence

$$\pi = PA v_1^\alpha v_2^\beta - P_1 v_1 - P_2 v_2$$

In order to maximise $\pi$ (or minimise it) $d\pi = 0$, therefore

$$d\pi = \alpha PA v_1^{\alpha-1} v_2^\beta dv_1 + \beta PA v_1^\alpha v_2^{\beta-1} dv_2 - P_1 dv_1 - P_2 dv_2 = 0 \tag{4.22}$$

that is

$$\left( \frac{\alpha Pq}{v_1} - P_1 \right) dv_1 + \left( \frac{\beta Pq}{v_2} - P_2 \right) dv_2 = 0$$

since this must be true for all values of $dv_1$, $dv_2$ it follows that:

$$\frac{\alpha Pq}{v_1} = P_1 \quad \text{and} \quad \frac{\beta Pq}{v_2} = P_2 \tag{4.23}$$

Since $\alpha Pq/v_1$ is the marginal revenue product of $v_1$ and $\beta Pq/v_2$ is that for $v_2$, (4.23) are the marginal productivity conditions.

The total income going to $v_1$ is $P_1 v_1$ and $= \alpha Pq$ and that going to

$v_2$ is $P_2 v_2$ and $= \beta P q$. Thus the factor shares, $P_1 v_1 / P_2 v_2 = \alpha/\beta$, hence are constant for all levels of output.

Also adding the income of $v_1$ to that of $v_2$ yields:

Factor income $= \alpha P q + \beta P q = (\alpha + \beta) P q$

Thus if returns to scale are increasing $(\alpha + \beta > 1)$ and factor incomes sum to more than national income $(Pq)$. When $\alpha + \beta = 1$, factor incomes exactly equal national income. When $\alpha + \beta < 1$, national income exceeds factor incomes. This is the adding up problem: since $Pq$ is the value added by capital and labour it should be exactly equal to the sum of factor shares.

These factor incomes are the minimum costs of producing output hence the optimum profit are:

$$\pi = Pq - (\alpha + \beta) Pq$$

Thus

$$\pi = Pq(1 - (\alpha + \beta))$$

Profits will be zero when $\alpha + \beta = 1$, negative when $\alpha + \beta > 1$ and positive when $\alpha + \beta < 1$. The adding up condition is tantamount to assuming $\alpha + \beta = 1$ and that profits are zero.

From (4.23) the optimum inputs are:

$$v_1^* = \frac{P \alpha q}{P_1}, \; v_2^* = \frac{P \beta q}{P_2}$$

putting these into the production function yields the profit maximising level of output:

$$q = A \left( \frac{P \alpha q}{P_1} \right)^\alpha \left( \frac{P \beta q}{P_2} \right)^\beta$$

$$q = q^{\alpha + \beta} A P^{\alpha + \beta} \left( \frac{\alpha}{P_1} \right)^\alpha \left( \frac{\beta}{P_2} \right)^\beta$$

If $\alpha + \beta = 1$, then it is obvious that we cannot find an optimum level of output since $q$ disappears from the equation.

These results are all posited on the assumption that the first order conditions (4.23) are those of a maximum, rather than a minimum, or a point of inflexion.

The second order conditions for a maximum are that $d^2 \pi < 0$, but from the appendix of Chapter 2 it is clear that this condition will be satisfied only when there are decreasing returns to scale. In this case positive profits are earned and optimum output is finite and determinate. When there are increasing returns to scale the first order conditions ensure a minimum and when there are constant returns to scale the first order conditions merely ensure that profits are zero.

This can perhaps be illustrated best with a diagram. See Figure 4.3. The minimum cost curve is horizontal for CRTS and hence when it lies above the demand curve (min cost (1)) it is impossible to equate MR to MC. At this level of cost no output would be produced thus reducing losses to a minimum. Similarly when minimum cost is below the demand curve (min cost (2)) it is still impossible to equate MC to MR but in this case a profit is made on each unit and hence output would be expanded to infinity. If MR is forced to equal MC then the MC curve lies on top of the MR curve and $\pi = 0$ and $q$ is indeterminate. The minimum cost curve is downward sloping when there are IRTS. Thus if it begins above the demand curve (min cost (2)) it, and its associated MC curve (MC1), will cut the demand curve from above (at $q_1$). This *minimises* profit. If the downward sloping cost curve begins *below* the demand curve then there will be no intersection of MC and MR. Minimum profit will occur at zero output and output goes to infinity for maximum profit.

The minimum cost curve is upward sloping when there are decreasing returns to scale. If it begins below the demand curve it, and

**FIGURE 4.3**

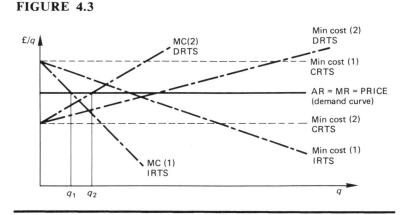

its associated MC curve will cut the demand curve. Output will be $q_2$ for maximum profits (all the conditions for a maximum are satisfied). If the minimum cost curve begins above the demand curve then there will be no intersection and losses will be minimised at zero output.

## 4.9   The Aggregate Cobb–Douglas Function

Much of the success with Cobb–Douglas functions was due to the results regarding distributive shares. When estimated on national income data, it was generally found that the values of $\beta$ and $\alpha$ were close to actual shares of labour and capital (0.7 for labour and 0.3 for capital). This indicated that the macro technology was of the Cobb–Douglas type, and that the Cobb–Douglas function accordingly was a true representation of macro technology. However, the macro Cobb–Douglas function was seriously questioned in the late 1960s by F. M. Fisher who conducted a series of simulations with the function. His general conclusion was:

> **An aggregate Cobb–Douglas *only* works well so long as labour's share is relatively constant. Where labour's share changes, predictions made with an aggregate Cobb–Douglas would cease to be good ones. This view is obviously correct, since an aggregate Cobb–Douglas predicts a constant share for labour. The point of our results, however, is not that an aggregate Cobb–Douglas fails to work well when labour's share ceases to be roughly constant, it is that an aggregate Cobb–Douglas function continues to work well so long as labour's share continues to be roughly constant, even though that rough constancy is not itself a consequence of the economy having a technology that is truly summarized by an aggregate Cobb–Douglas . . . [though] interesting descriptive and empirical devices . . . our result damages the view that the apparent success of aggregate production functions in wage predictions shows that the true technological relationships of a diverse economy can really be summarized for theoretical purposes in an aggregate production function.**

Really, Fisher's result was not surprising. The production function is a micro concept, and we cannot expect that a micro concept can also be used in macro studies.

Consider for example an economy comprising two sectors each of which is representable by a Cobb–Douglas function i.e.

$$q_1 = AK_1^\alpha L_1^\beta$$

and

$$q_2 = AK_2^\alpha L_2^\beta$$

for ease of expression we assume the functions are identical.

$q_i$ is the output of sector $i$
$K_i$ is the capital of sector $i$
$L_i$ is the labour of sector $i$

In aggregate we have:

$$(q_1 + q_2) = A(K_1^\alpha L_1^\beta + K_2^\alpha L_2^\beta)$$

which is not an aggregate Cobb–Douglas, that is it is not

$$(q_1 + q_2) = A(K_1 + K_2)^\alpha (L_1 + L_2)^\beta$$

If, however, the factors in the two sectors remain in fixed proportions we can write $K_1 = \lambda_1 K_2$ and $L_1 = \lambda_2 L_2$, hence

$$(q_1 + q_2) = A(\lambda_1 K_2)^\alpha (\lambda_2 L_2)^\beta + K_2^\alpha L_2^\beta$$

therefore

$$(q_1 + q_2) = AK_2^\alpha L_2^\beta (\lambda_1^\alpha + \lambda_2^\beta + 1)$$

Hence the aggregate would behave as a Cobb–Douglas but if $\lambda_1$ and/or $\lambda_2$ changes then the function is no longer a Cobb–Douglas. Thus the conditions necessary for a Cobb–Douglas to exist at the process level, the firm level, the industry level and the national level are rather severe.

The possibility of fitting a Cobb–Douglas function to national accounting data generated by quite strange production functions has been demonstrated graphically by von Shaik (1974). He shows that points in the $v_1 v_2$ space shown in Figure 4.4 will also yield a 'Cobb–Douglas' set of observations. But see Solow (1974) for a critical comment.

**FIGURE 4.4**

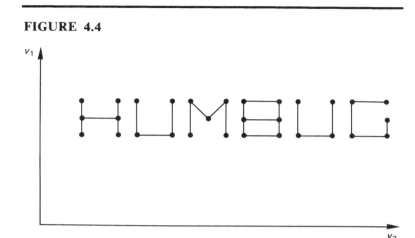

## Selected Reading

The Cobb–Douglas function was presented in C. W. Cobb and P. H. Douglas, 'A Theory of Production' (1928) (*American Economic Review*, supp. XXIII pp. 139–65). On the history of the function and its early development, see P. H. Douglas, 'Are there Laws of Production?' (1948) (*The American Economic Review*, XXXVIII) and P. H. Douglas, 'Comments on the Cobb–Douglas Production Function' (1967), in M. Brown (ed.), *The Theory and Empirical Analysis of Production*.

For a modern discussion of its properties, see C. E. Ferguson, '*The Neoclassical Theory of Production and Distribution*' (1969) pp. 163–6. The aggregate Cobb–Douglas function was tested by F. M. Fisher who reported the results in 'Aggregate Production Function and the Explanation of Wages: A Simulation Experiment' (1971), *Review of Economics and Statistics*, LIII. Its usefulness was questioned by A. von Shaik, 'Laws of Production and Laws of Algebra: The Humbug Production Function' (1974), *Review of Economics and Statistics*. For a rebuttal of this see R. M. Solow, 'Laws of Production and Laws of Algebra: The Humbug Production Function: A comment' (1974), *Review of Economics and Statistics*.

# The CES Function

## 5.1 Generalising the Cobb–Douglas

The first step in the development of the production function had been taken by Cobb and Douglas in the 1920s. The second step was to come some forty years later by a quartet of economists – Arrow, Chenery, Minhas and Solow (ACMS). They developed the Constant Elasticity of Substitution function.

The CES function was invoked by ACMS in response to an empirical test they carried out to see if the factor rewards were indeed constant as implied by the Cobb–Douglas function or whether some more general function would fit the data better.

The test they proposed was derived from the first order conditions of the Cobb–Douglas function with perfectly competitive markets. Using the product price as the numeraire we have:

$$\pi = A v_1^\alpha v_2^\beta - P_1 v_1 - P_2 v_2$$

$$\frac{\partial \pi}{\partial v_1} = A \alpha v_1^{\alpha-1} v_2^\beta - P_1 = 0$$

Hence

$$\frac{\alpha q}{v_1} = P_1 \tag{5.1}$$

Thus according to Cobb–Douglas the average product of a factor $[q/v_1]$ is a constant proportion of its price ($P_1$).

ACMS proposed a slightly more general relationship of the form:

$$\frac{q}{v_1} = \left(\frac{P_1}{\alpha}\right)^{\lambda} \tag{5.2}$$

They used cross-sectional data for 24 industries drawn from various countries to test the restriction (implied by Cobb–Douglas) that $\lambda = 1$. They found that $\lambda$ was significantly different from 1 in most cases and hence that the Cobb–Douglas function was not an adequate description of the data generating process.

These empirical findings led to attempts to derive a mathematical function having the properties of (a) homogeneity, (b) constant elasticity of substitution between capital and labour, and (c) the possibilities of different elasticities for different industries.

The function which was found to give rise to (5.2) has the form:

$$q^{-\theta} = \gamma^{-\theta}(\delta v_1^{-\theta} + (1-\delta)v_2^{-\theta}) \tag{5.3}$$

and this is the usual way of writing the CES function. It can of course be generalized to include more than two inputs:

$$q^{-\theta} = \gamma^{-\theta}(\alpha_1 v_1^{-\theta} + \alpha_2 v_2^{-\theta} + \dots \alpha_n v_n^{-\theta}) \tag{5.4}$$

where $\Sigma_n \alpha_n = 1$.

Now, profit ($\pi$) are defined to be $\pi \equiv q - P_1 v_1 - P_2 v_2$. ($P$ is the numeraire) hence, using (5.3), the profit function becomes:

$$\pi = \gamma[\delta v_1^{-\theta} + (1-\delta)v_2^{-\theta}]^{-(1/\theta)} - P_1 v_1 - P_2 v_2$$

and a first order condition for a maximum is:

$$\frac{\partial \pi}{\partial v_1} = \frac{\gamma}{\theta}(\delta v_1^{-\theta} + (1-\delta)v_2^{-\theta})^{-(1/\theta)-1}(-\theta \delta v_1^{-\theta-1}) - P_1 = 0$$

Therefore

$$\gamma\left(\frac{q}{\gamma}\right)^{\theta(1/\theta+1)} \delta v_1^{-(\theta+1)} = P_1$$

Therefore

$$\left(\frac{q}{v_1}\right)^{\theta+1} = \frac{P_1}{\delta}\gamma^{\theta}$$

Therefore

$$\frac{q}{v_1} = \left(\frac{P_1 \gamma^{\theta}}{\delta}\right)^{1/\theta+1} \tag{5.5}$$

It is clear that (5.5) is equivalent to (5.2) with $\lambda = 1/\theta + 1$ and hence (5.3) is a functional form suitable for representing the data generating process.

Since the CES is claimed to contain the Cobb–Douglas as a special case it should be possible to derive the Cobb–Douglas from (5.3) by imposing some restrictions on its parameters. Equation (5.5) suggests that for the CES to become Cobb–Douglas, it is necessary to restrict $\theta$ to zero. Unfortunately, if this is put into (5.3) the equation collapses. The solution is therefore by way of L'Hospital's rule.

Differentiating (5.3) w.r.t. $\theta$ yields:

$$-q^{-\theta}\log q = -\delta(\gamma v_1)^{-\theta}\log(\gamma v_1) - (1-\delta)(\gamma v_2)^{-\theta}\log(\gamma v_2)$$

Putting $\theta = 0$ yields:

$$\log q = \delta\log(\gamma v_1) + (1-\delta)\log(\gamma v_2)$$

$$\underline{q = \gamma v_1^{\delta}v_2^{(1-\delta)}}$$

which is Cobb–Douglas with constant returns to scale. Thus the CES does reduce to a CD when $\theta = 0$, that is when $\lambda = 1$

## 5.2   The Elasticity of Substitution of the CES

The elasticity of substitution ($\sigma$) has already been defined as:

$$\sigma = \frac{\mathrm{d}(v_1/v_2)}{(v_1/v_2)} \Big/ \frac{\mathrm{d}(\mathrm{d}v_1/\mathrm{d}v_2)}{(\mathrm{d}v_1/\mathrm{d}v_2)} \tag{5.6}$$

Differentiating (5.3), the CES function, yields, for $q = \bar{q}$:

$$0 = -\gamma^{-\theta}\theta\delta v_1^{-\theta-1}\mathrm{d}v_1 - \gamma^{-\theta}\theta(1-\delta)v_2^{-\theta-1}\mathrm{d}v_2$$

hence

$$\frac{\mathrm{d}v_1}{\mathrm{d}v_2} = -\frac{(1-\delta)}{\delta}\left(\frac{v_1}{v_2}\right)^{\theta+1} \tag{5.7}$$

Differentiating (5.7) w.r.t. $(v_1/v_2)$ yields

$$\frac{\mathrm{d}(\mathrm{d}v_1/\mathrm{d}v_2)}{\mathrm{d}(v_1/v_2)} = -\frac{(1-\delta)}{\delta}(\theta+1)\left(\frac{v_1}{v_2}\right)^{\theta} \tag{5.8}$$

Substituting (5.7) and (5.8) into (5.6) yields

$$\sigma = \left(\frac{v_1}{v_2}\right)^{\theta+1} \left(\frac{1}{\theta+1}\right) \left(\frac{v_2}{v_1}\right)^{-\theta} \left(\frac{v_2}{v_1}\right)^{-1}$$

Therefore

$$\sigma = \frac{1}{\theta+1} \tag{5.9}$$

Thus the elasticity of substitution of the CES function is constant, as its name implies, and depends entirely on one of the parameters of the production function, that is $\theta$.

Note (5.5), the equation tested by ACMS, can now be rewritten as

$$\frac{q}{v_1} = \left(\frac{P_1 \gamma^{\theta}}{\delta}\right)^{\sigma}$$

from which it is immediately clear that the relationship between a factor's average product $(q/v_1)$ and its price $(P_1)$ depends on the elasticity of substitution of the underlying production function $(\sigma)$.

## 5.3.  The CES Isoquants

The slope of the isoquant can be derived from equation (5.7)

$$\frac{dv_1}{dv_2} = -\frac{(1-\delta)}{\delta} \left(\frac{v_1}{v_2}\right)^{\theta+1}$$

It is negatively sloped for $0 < \delta < 1$ and the slope varies with $(v_1/v_2)$. Along any given ray $(\bar{v}_1/\bar{v}_2)$ the slope of each successive isoquant is the same hence the CES is homothetic.

The slope varies along the isoquant depending on the elasticity of substitution. For example when

$$\theta = -1, \quad \sigma = \frac{1}{\theta+1} = \infty \quad \text{and} \quad \frac{dv_1}{dv_2} = \frac{-(1-\delta)}{\delta}$$

hence the isoquant is a straight line of slope $-(1-\delta)/\delta$ and the inputs are perfect substitutes.

Alternatively for $\theta = \infty$, $\sigma = 1/\theta+1 = 0$ and

$$\frac{dv_1}{dv_2} = \infty \quad \text{when} \quad \frac{v_1}{v_2} > 1 \quad \text{and} \quad 0 \text{ when } \frac{v_1}{v_2} < 1.$$

Hence the isoquant is rectangular with its corner on the 45° line $(v_1/v_2 = 1)$. For all $(v_1/v_2)$ above the 45° line the isoquant is vertical and for all $(v_1/v_2)$ below the 45° line the isoquant is horizontal. The inputs are therefore perfect complements when the elasticity of substitution is zero. Notice that when this is the case the factors must be used in equal quantities.

Between these extremes, of $\sigma = 0$ and $\sigma = \infty$, there is a whole range of possible $\sigma$'s.

(i) When $\theta = 0$, $\sigma = 1$ we have the Cobb–Douglas case and

$$\frac{dv_1}{dv_2} = \frac{(1-\delta)}{\delta}\left(\frac{v_1}{v_2}\right)$$

which as already shown in Chapter 4 is asymptotic to the axes.

(ii) For $\sigma < 1$, the isoquants are asymptotic to particular levels of $v_1$ and $v_2$ and for $\sigma > 1$ they intercept the axes.

These asymptotes and intercepts can be found by allowing $v_1$ and/or $v_2$ to go to either zero of infinity, thus

from (5.3) $\qquad q^{-\theta} = \gamma^{-\theta}\delta v_1^{-\theta} + \gamma^{-\theta}(1-\delta)v_2^{-\theta}$

For given $q$ and $-1 < \theta < 0$ when $v_2 \to 0$; $\overline{q}^{-\theta} = \gamma^{-\theta}\delta v_1^{-\theta}$
Therefore

$$v_1 = \frac{(\delta)^{1/\theta}}{\gamma}q$$

which is the isoquant's *intercept* on the $v_1$ axis.

For given $q$ and $0 < \theta < \infty$ letting $v_2 \to \infty$; $\overline{q}^{-\theta} = \gamma^{-\theta}\delta v_1^{-\theta}$. Therefore again

$$v_1 = \frac{(\delta)^{1/\theta}}{\gamma}q$$

but in this case it is the level of $v_1$ to which the isoquant asymptotically approaches as $v_2 \to \infty$.

These isoquants, their intercepts and asymptotes are shown in Figure 5.1.

*Note.* This function is *strictly* convex only when $\sigma \leqslant 1$. When the axes are intercepted then the function is convex but not strictly convex.

These isoquants are drawn for (a) $\sigma = 0$ (the fixed coefficient or 'Leontief' case); (b) $\sigma = 1$ (the Cobb–Douglas case which has the axes as asymptotes; and (c) $\sigma = \infty$ ($v_1$ and $v_2$ are perfect substitutes).

**FIGURE 5.1**

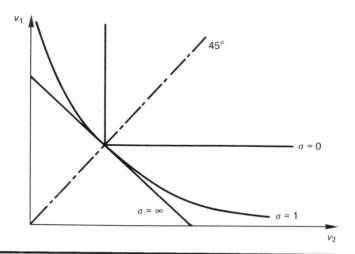

For all isoquants with elasticities of substitution between 0 and 1 the horizontal asymptote will be

$$v_1 \to \frac{(\delta)^{1/\theta}}{\gamma}\,\bar{q} \qquad \text{as } v_2 \to \infty.$$

The vertical asymptote will be

$$v_2 \to \frac{(1-\delta)^{1/\theta}}{\gamma}\,\bar{q} \qquad \text{as } v_1 \to \infty.$$

For all isoquants with elasticities of substitution between 1 and $\infty$ the intercept on the $v_2$ axis will be $(1-\delta)^{1/\theta}/\gamma\,\bar{q}$ and that of the $v_1$ axis will be $[(\delta)^{1/\theta}/\gamma]\bar{q}$.

## 5.4  Returns to Scale

Returns to scale are defined as the ratio of the proportionate change in output to the proportionate change in inputs when all inputs change by the same proportion.

From the CES we have:

$$q^{-\theta} = \gamma^{-\theta}\delta v_1^{-\theta} + \gamma^{-\theta}(1-\delta)v_2^{-\theta}$$

Total differentiation yields:

$$-\theta dq \cdot q^{-\theta-1} = -\theta\gamma^{-\theta}\delta v_1^{-\theta-1}\,dv_1 - \theta\gamma^{-\theta}(1-\delta)v_2^{-\theta-1}\,dv_2$$

Dividing by $-\theta$ and rearranging:

$$\frac{dq}{q}q^{-\theta} = \gamma^{-\theta}\delta v_1^{-\theta}\frac{dv_1}{v_1} + \gamma^{-\theta}(1-\delta)v_2^{-\theta}\frac{dv_2}{v_2}$$

Assuming

$$\frac{dv_1}{v_1} = \frac{dv_2}{v_2} = \frac{dv}{v},$$

yields

$$\frac{dq}{q}q^{-\theta} = \frac{dv}{v}\left(\gamma^{-\theta}\delta v_1^{-\theta} + \gamma^{-\theta}(1-\delta)v_2^{-\theta}\right)$$

therefore

$$\underline{\frac{dq}{q}\bigg/\frac{dv}{v} = 1}$$

Thus the CES, as specified by ACMS, has constant returns to scale everywhere. Thus, like the CRTS Cobb–Douglas function, the long-run average cost and marginal cost curves are horizontal rather than 'U'-shaped.

A more general specification of the CES would be:

$$q^{-\delta/\mu} = \gamma^{-\theta}\delta v_1^{-\theta} + \gamma^{-\theta}(1-\delta)v_2^{-\theta} \qquad (5.10)$$

This, too, has a constant elasticity of substitution of $1/1+\theta$ but has returns to scale $\mu$. Thus returns to scale are everywhere the same, once $\mu$ is specified, but can be increasing, decreasing or constant ($\mu > 1$, $\mu < 1$, $\mu = 1$ respectively).

### 5.5 Short-run Total, Average and Marginal Products for the CES

#### SR Total product

The short run is defined to be that period during which one input is deemed to be fixed. Let this be $v_1$ fixed at $\bar{v}_1$. From (5.3) we have:

$$q^{-\theta} = \gamma^{-\theta}\delta\bar{v}_1^{-\theta} + \gamma^{-\theta}(1-\delta)v_2^{-\theta}$$

or

$$q^{-\theta} = B + \gamma^{-\theta}(1-\delta)v_2^{-\theta}$$

where $B = \gamma^{-\theta}\delta\bar{v}_1^{-\theta}$ (a constant by assumption)
or

$$q = v_2 \left[ Bv_2^\theta + \gamma^{-\theta}(1-\delta) \right]^{-(1/\theta)} \tag{5.11}$$

(5.11) is the equation for the total product of $v_2$, say labour. It may also be thought of as the short-run or *ex post* production function since it represents the whole choice set of production possibilities open to an existing business in the short run.

### SR average product

Some possible shapes for (5.11) are shown in Figure 5.2. $v_2$ is always productive (i.e. $q$ is an increasing function of $v_2$) but becomes less and less productive as output grows. This can be seen from the average product curve for $v_2$.

$$\mathrm{AP}v_2 = \left(\frac{q}{v_2}\right) = \left[ B v_2^\theta + \gamma^{-\theta}(1-\delta) \right]^{-(1/\theta)} \tag{5.12}$$

This will be positive for all $0 \leqslant \delta \leqslant 1$ and will decline as $v_2$ increases, since:

$$\frac{\mathrm{dAP}v_2}{\mathrm{d}v_2} = -\frac{1}{\theta}\left[ Bv_2^\theta + \gamma^{-\theta}(1-\delta) \right]^{-(1/\theta)-1}\theta Bv_2^{\theta-1} < 0 \tag{5.13}$$

### SR marginal product

The marginal product of $v_2$ is found by taking the partial derivative of $q$ w.r.t. $v_2$. From (5.11) we obtain:

$$\mathrm{MP}v_2 = \frac{\mathrm{d}q}{\mathrm{d}v_2} = \gamma^{-\theta}(1-\delta)\left(\frac{q}{v_2}\right)^{1+\theta} \tag{5.14}$$

Thus the $\mathrm{MP}v_2$ is positive when $0 < \delta < 1$ and unambiguously declines with $v_2$ since we have already shown (5.13) that $[q/v_2]$ declines with $v_2$.

This last remark also requires of course that $\theta$ does not go below $-1$ but since the elasticity of substitution has a possible range of 0 to $\infty$ this implies a possible range of $\theta$ between $\infty$ and $-1$.

**FIGURE 5.2**
**Illustration to Three Different CES Short-run Functions**

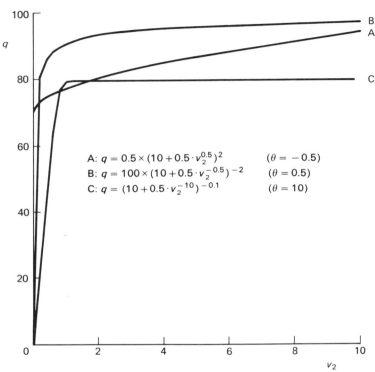

A: $q = 0.5 \times (10 + 0.5 \cdot v_2^{0.5})^2$      $(\theta = -0.5)$

B: $q = 100 \times (10 + 0.5 \cdot v_2^{-0.5})^{-2}$      $(\theta = 0.5)$

C: $q = (10 + 0.5 \cdot v_2^{-10})^{-0.1}$      $(\theta = 10)$

Thus, for reasonable assumptions, the CES function obeys the law of diminishing returns and its SR marginal product curve is downward sloping.

## 5.6 The CES Factor Demand Functions

Factor demand functions relate the demand for factor inputs to their prices and to the level of output. They are derived by assuming some optimisation by the entrepreneur and for current purposes this optimisation means maximising profits.

Profits are defined as:

$$\pi = Pq - P_1 v_1 - P_2 v_2$$

for a max, and assuming perfectly competitive markets, it is necessary that:

$$\frac{\partial \pi}{\partial v_1} = P \frac{\partial q}{\partial v_1} dv_1 - P_1 dv_1 = 0$$

$$\frac{\partial \pi}{\partial v_2} = P \frac{\partial q}{\partial v_1} dv_2 - P_1 dv_2 = 0$$

(5.15)

Thus

$$\frac{\partial q}{\partial v_1} = \frac{P_1}{P}; \quad \frac{\partial q}{\partial v_2} = \frac{P_2}{P}$$

(5.16)

(5.16) are the first order or marginal productivity conditions – the marginal revenue product of a factor $[(\partial q/\partial v_i)P]$ is equal to its price $(P_i)$.

From (5.10) we have:

$$q^{-\theta/\mu} = \gamma^{-\theta} \delta v_1^{-\theta} + \gamma^{-\theta}(1-\delta)v_2^{-\theta}$$

Thus

$$\frac{\partial q}{\partial v_1} = \mu q^{1 + (\theta/\mu)} \gamma^{-\theta} \delta \bar{v}_1^{\theta - 1}$$

Substituting (5.16) and rearranging yields

$$v_1 = (\mu \delta q^{\theta/\mu + 1} \gamma^{-\theta} P_1^{-1} P)^\sigma$$

(5.17)

and, by symmetry:

$$v_2 = (\mu(1-\delta)q^{\theta/\mu + 1} \gamma^{-\theta} P_2^{-1} P)^\sigma$$

From (5.17)

$$\frac{v_1}{v_2} = \left( \frac{\delta P_2}{(1-\delta)P_1} \right)^\sigma$$

Thus substituting this in (5.10) yields

$$q^{-\theta/\mu} = \gamma^{-\theta} \left[ \delta v_2^{-\theta} \left( \frac{\delta P_2}{(1-\delta)P_1} \right)^{-\sigma\theta} + (1-\delta)v_2^{-\theta} \right]$$

$$q^{-\theta/\mu} = \gamma^{-\theta} v_2^{-\theta} (1 - \delta) \left[ \left( \frac{\delta}{1 - \delta} \right)^{\sigma} \left( \frac{P_2}{P_1} \right)^{-\sigma\theta} + 1 \right]$$

therefore

$$v_2 = \frac{q^{1/\mu}}{\gamma} (1 - \delta)^{1/\theta} \left[ \left( \frac{\delta}{1 - \delta} \right)^{\sigma} \left( \frac{P_1}{P_2} \right)^{\sigma\theta} + 1 \right]^{1/\theta} \qquad (5.18(a))$$

This expresses the demand for $v_2$ in terms of output and relative factor prices. It is the factor demand equation,

By symmetry:

$$v_1 = \frac{q^{1/\mu}}{\gamma} (\delta)^{1/\theta} \left[ \left( \frac{1 - \delta}{\delta} \right)^{\sigma} \left( \frac{P_2}{P_1} \right)^{\sigma\theta} + 1 \right]^{1/\theta} \qquad (5.18(b))$$

With constant returns to scale $\mu = 1$ and the demand for inputs is proportional to output. The effect of relative prices, however, depends upon the elasticity of substitution $(\sigma)$. When $\sigma = 0$ the inputs are perfect complements and hence prices have no effect on factor demands. This is the Leontief case of fixed coefficients. When $\sigma = \infty$ the inputs are perfect substitutes and very small changes in relative prices can switch from using only $v_1$ to using only $v_2$.

These results are derived from the first order conditions but as shown in Chapter 2 the second order conditions are satisfied only when there are decreasing returns to scale (or imperfect competition).

Imposing the 1st order conditions with CRTS and perfectly competitive markets merely ensures that profits are everywhere zero and this is brought about by the whole industry reaching its optimum size. Thus imposing these conditions is tantamount to imposing long run equilibrium. These factor demand equations exist only when $\partial q / \partial v_1$ and $\partial q / \partial v_2$ exist. As we have seen, the isoquants of the CES cut the axes for $\infty \geqslant \sigma > 1$ and the factor demand functions exist only over the domain $v_1 > 0$, $v_2 > 0$.

## 5.7 CES Cost Functions

The cost function is the dual of the production function and expresses total cost in terms of output and factor prices. Once again the basis of this function is profit maximisation in perfectly competitive markets.

We have defined cost as:

$$C = P_1 v_1 + P_2 v_2 \qquad (5.19)$$

Substituting the factor demand equations (5.18) into (5.19) yields:

$$C = q^{1/\mu}\gamma^{-1}\left\{(1-\delta)^{1/\theta}\left[\left(\frac{\delta}{(1-\delta)}\right)^{\sigma}\left(\frac{P_1}{P_2}\right)^{\sigma\theta}+1\right]^{1/\theta}P_2\right.$$

$$\left.+\delta^{1/\theta}\left[\left(\frac{1-\delta}{\delta}\right)^{\sigma}\left(\frac{P_2}{P_1}\right)^{\sigma\theta}+1\right]^{1/\theta}P_1\right\}$$

After some intricate and tedious manipulation this becomes:

$$C = q^{1/\mu}\gamma^{-1}P_1P_2\left[(1-\delta)^{\sigma}P_1^{-\sigma\theta}+\delta^{\sigma}P_2^{-\sigma\theta}\right]^{1/\sigma\theta} \tag{5.20}$$

This is very similar indeed to its 'dual', the CES production function. It is, however, homogeneous of degree one in prices. If $P_1$ and $P_2$ are multiplied by some factor $n$ then:

$$C_2 = q^{1/\mu}\gamma^{-1}P_1P_2n^2\left[(1-\delta)^{\sigma}P_1^{-\sigma0}n^{-\sigma\theta}+\delta^{\sigma}P_2^{-\sigma\theta}n^{-\sigma\theta}\right]^{1/\sigma\theta}$$

therefore $C_2 = nC_1$

Thus cost increases *pari passu* with prices. When the underlying production function is of constant returns to scale ($\mu = 1$) then costs do not vary with output. When $\mu > 1$ average cost decreases with $q$ and when $\mu < 1$ average cost increases with $q$.

The Cost Function can be used to derive the factor demand equations.

From the CES cost function (5.20) we have:

$$\frac{\partial C}{\partial P_1} = q^{1/\mu}\gamma^{-1}P_2\left\{[(1-\delta)^{\sigma}P_1^{-\sigma\theta}+\delta^{\sigma}P_2^{-\sigma\theta}]^{1/\sigma\theta}\right.$$

$$\left.-P_1[(1-\delta)^{\sigma}P_1^{-\sigma\theta}+\delta^{\sigma}P_2^{-\sigma\theta}]^{1/\sigma\theta-1}P_1^{-\sigma\theta-1}(1-\delta)^{\sigma}\right\}$$

$$= q^{1/\mu}\gamma^{-1}\left\{\left[(1-\delta)^{\sigma}\left(\frac{P_2}{P_1}\right)^{\sigma\theta}+\delta^{\sigma}\right]^{1/\sigma\theta}\right.$$

$$\left.-\left(\frac{P_2}{P_1}\right)^{\sigma\theta}(1-\delta)^{\sigma}\left[(1-\delta)^{\sigma}\left(\frac{P_2}{P_1}\right)^{\sigma\theta}+\delta^{\sigma}\right]^{1/\sigma\theta-1}\right\}$$

$$= q^{1/\mu}\gamma^{-1}\left[(1-\delta)^{\sigma}\left(\frac{P_2}{P_1}\right)^{\sigma\theta}+\delta^{\sigma}\right]^{(1/\theta\sigma)-1}$$

$$\left[(1-\delta)^{\sigma}\left(\frac{P_2}{P_1}\right)^{\sigma\theta}+\delta^{\sigma}-\left(\frac{P_2}{P_1}\right)^{\sigma\theta}(1-\delta)^{\sigma}\right]$$

$$\frac{\partial C}{\partial P_1} = q^{1/\mu}\gamma^{-1}\delta^{1/\theta}\left[\left(\frac{1-\delta}{\delta}\right)^{\sigma}\left(\frac{P_2}{P_1}\right)^{\sigma\theta}+1\right]^{1/\theta}$$

This is identical to the CES factor demand equations (5.18) demonstrating once again the Shephard result that differentiating the cost function w.r.t. a factor price yields the cost minimising level of input of that factor.

## Selected Reading

The CES production function was introduced by Dickinson in *Review of Economic Studies* (1954) and popularised in a joint article by K. J. Arrow, H. B. Chenery, B. S. Minhas and R. M. Solow: 'Capital and Labour Substitution and Economic Efficiency' (1961), *Review of Economics and Statistics*, xliii, pp. 225–34. A good summary of the history and early development is given in M. Nerlove, 'Recent Empirical Studies of the CES and Related Production Functions' (1967), in M. Brown (ed.), *The Theory and Empirical Analysis of Production*.

# The Translog Function

## 6.1 Introduction

The CES was a natural extension of the Cobb–Douglas in that it permitted the elasticity of substitution to be something other than unity. The next obvious step is to generate a function which allows the elasticity of substitution to change with output and/or factor proportions.

A rather different kind of generalisation also suggests itself. For both the CES and the CD functions the elasticity of scale (returns to scale) were fixed. That is to say if the elasticity of scale was '$n$' for one level of output and one factor combination then it will be '$n$' for all levels of output and all factor combinations. This results in the long-run average cost curve which is either continuously rising, a horizontal line or continuously falling. Thus the LRAC curve cannot take the 'U'-shape so often assumed for it in the theory of the firm. The second generalisation is therefore to allow the elasticity of scale to change with output and/or factor proportions.

One such general function is the so-called Translog Production Function. This is a contraction of Transcendental Logarithmic Function. By transcendental is meant non-algebraic and logarithmic functions are one form of transcendental function.

For the two-input case the function is:

$$\log q = \log \gamma_0 + \alpha_1 \log v_1 + \beta_1 \log v_2 + \alpha_2 (\log v_1)^2$$
$$+ \beta_2 (\log v_2)^2 + \gamma_1 \log v_1 \log v_1 \tag{6.1}$$

**105**

In general:

$$\log q = \log \gamma_0 + \sum_i \alpha_i \log v_i$$

$$+ \frac{1}{2} \sum_i \sum_j \beta_{ij} \log v_j \log v_i \qquad (6.2)$$

where $\beta_{ij} = \beta_{ji}$ for all $i, j$.

This function has become enormously popular and originated in Christensen *et al.* (1971) (see also Christensen *et al.*, 1973).

A logarithmic function can, in principle, be derived from any 'normal' (algebraic) production function since any point in the $(v_1 v_2)$ space can be uniquely mapped into a point in the $(\log v_1, \log v_2)$ space. Thus for any algebraic function there must exist a logarithmic version.

There is an important caveat here. It was shown in Chapter 5 that the CES function includes the points $v_1 = 0$ and $v_2 = 0$ even when output is not zero. (This is true at the intercepts when $1 < \sigma \leqslant \infty$.) There is no logarithmic equivalent of zero and so transposing points in the $(v_1 v_2)$ space into the $(\log v_1, \log v_2)$ space necessarily excludes the corner solutions. It is arguable that this is a small price to pay since we are rarely interested in such extremes.

The translog function may be regarded as a production function in its own right or as a Taylor series expansion in two steps of an arbitrary function:

$$y = f(z_1, z_2 \ldots z_n) \qquad (6.3)$$

Let its partial derivatives be $f_i$ and $f_{ij}$ at a point $z_1 = a_1$, $z_2 = a_2, \ldots, z_n = a_n$. The function $f(z)$ can then be approximated in the neighbourhood $(x_i)$ of $(a_1, a_2, \ldots, a_n)$ with the following expression:

$$f(a_1 + x_1, a_2 + x_2, \ldots, a_n + x_n)$$
$$= f(a_1, a_2, \ldots, a_n) + x_1 f_1 + x_2 f_2 + \ldots + x_n f_n$$
$$+ 1/2 \cdot [x_1^2 f_{11} + \ldots + x_n^2 f_{nn}$$
$$+ 2x_1 x_2 f_1 f_{12} + 2x_1 x_3 f_{13} + \ldots + 2x_{n-1} x_n f_{n,n-1}] + R_n$$

where $R_n$ is a 'remainder term' and the partial derivatives $f_i$ and $f_{ij}$ are to be evaluated at the point $a_1, a_2, \ldots, a_n$. The expression above is called a Taylor's expansion in two steps of $f(z)$ around the point

$a_1, a_2, \ldots, a_n$. If we know that the remainder term is 'small' (which it normally is for well behaved functions and for small values of $(x_1, x_2, \ldots, x_n)$) we could drop that term.

Assume now that we wanted to study the function in the neighbourhood of the point $0, 0, \ldots, 0$. Assuming a vanishing remainder term, we have

$$
\begin{aligned}
y = f(z_1, z_2, \ldots, z_n) \\
= f(0) + z_1 f_1(0) + \ldots + z_n f_n(0) + 1/2[z_1^2 f_{11}(0) + \ldots \\
+ 2z_{n-1} z_n f_{n-1,n}(0)]
\end{aligned} \tag{6.4}
$$

Accordingly, we have a linear expansion of the function $f(z)$ near origin. If we estimated this function with the equation $y = b_0 + b_1 z_1 + \ldots b_n z_n + b_{11} z_1^2 + \ldots + b_{nn} z_n^2 + \ldots + b_{n-1,n} z_{n-1} z_n$ we would obviously obtain $b_0 = f(0)$, $b_1 = f_1(0), \ldots, b_{n-1,n} = f_{n-1,n}(0)$. If now $z_i = \ln(v_i)$ $i = 1, \ldots, n$, the point $z = 0$ corresponds to the point $v = 1$. Thus, we can say that the expansion (6.4) occurs around the point $v_1 = v_2 \ldots = v_n = 1$.

It is easily seen that the expansion (6.4) corresponds to our formulation of the translog production function in (6.2) (with $f(0) = \ln a_1, f_i(0) = b_i, z_i = \ln v_i$ etc.). Thus we conclude that the translog production function can be regarded as a Taylor expansion in two steps of an arbitrary function (6.3), around the point $v_1 = v_2 = \ldots = v_n = 1$.

## 6.2 The Elasticity of Scale and the Translog

The elasticity of scale ($\varepsilon$) can be found by taking the total differential of the function, thus:

$$
\log q = \log \gamma_0 + \alpha_1 \log v_1 + \beta_1 \log v_2 \\
+ \alpha_2 (\log v_1)^2 + \beta_2 (\log v_2)^2 + \gamma_1 (\log v_1 \log v_2)
$$

becomes:

$$
\frac{dq}{q} = \alpha_1 \frac{dv_1}{v_1} + \beta_1 \frac{dv_2}{v_2} + 2\alpha_2 \log v_1 \frac{dv_1}{v_1} + 2\beta_2 \log v_2 \frac{dv_2}{v_2} \\
+ \gamma_1 \log v_1 \frac{dv_2}{v_2} + \gamma_1 \log v_2 \frac{dv_1}{v_1} \tag{6.5}
$$

Therefore, since

$$\frac{dv_1}{v_1} = \frac{dv_2}{v_2} = \frac{dv}{v}$$

$$\varepsilon = \frac{dq}{q} \bigg/ \frac{dv}{v} = \alpha_1 + \beta_1 + 2\alpha_2 \log v_1 + 2\beta_2 \log v_2$$

$$+ \gamma_1 \log v_1 + \gamma_1 \log v_2$$

$$\varepsilon = \alpha_1 + \beta_1 + (2\alpha_2 + \gamma_1) \log v_1 + (2\beta_2 + \gamma_1) \log v_2 \qquad (6.6)$$

From this it is clear that in general the elasticity of scale changes with factor proportions and with the level of production.

The elasticity of scale can be rendered independent of the level of production (but dependent on factor proportions) if $\alpha_1 = -\beta_2$ in which case:

$$\varepsilon = \alpha_1 + \beta_1 + (2\alpha_2 + \gamma_1)\left[ \log\left(\frac{v_1}{v_2}\right) \right]$$

It is clear from (6.6) that $\varepsilon$ may be rendered independent of $v_1$ by constraining $2\alpha_2 = -\gamma_1$ and independent of $v_2$ by constraining $2\beta_2 = -\gamma_1$.

The elasticity may be rendered independent of $v_1$ and $v_2$ altogether by constraining $\gamma_1 = -2\alpha_2 = -2\beta_2$ in which case $\varepsilon$ is unchanging at $(\alpha_1 + \beta_1)$. For this to be further constrained to constant returns to scale then $\alpha_1 + \beta_1 = 1$.

Therefore the elasticity of scale has in general to be calculated for each point $(v_1, v_2)$ on the production function. However, some rather simple constraints may be imposed to ensure the desired elasticity of scale can be achieved.

If the restrictions for constant returns to scale are imposed on the translog function it becomes:

$$\log q = \log \gamma_0 + \log v_1 + \beta_1 \log\left(\frac{v_2}{v_1}\right)$$

$$+ \beta_2 \{(\log v_1)^2 - 2 \log v_1 \log v_2 + (\log v_2)^2\}$$

Therefore

$$\log\left(\frac{q}{v_1}\right) = \log \gamma_0 + \beta_1 \log\left(\frac{v_2}{v_1}\right) + \beta_2 \cdot \left[ \log\left(\frac{v_2}{v_1}\right) \right]^2 \qquad (6.7)$$

Equation (6.7) is of particular interest because it is the Taylor expansion of the CES function. This version of the CES was first suggested by Kmenta and hence is known as the Kmenta approximation. The derivation of the Kmenta approximation is given in the appendix to Chapter 7. It is mentioned here merely to point out that constraining the translog function to have constant returns to scale is tantamount to using a CES function.

## 6.3 The Translog Isoquant

The shape of the isoquant can be obtained by fixing output at $\bar{q}$ and differentiating it using (6.5). With $dq = 0$, we obtain:

$$\frac{dv_2}{dv_1} = -\frac{v_2}{v_1}\left\{\frac{\alpha_1 + 2\alpha_2 \log v_1 + \gamma_1 \log v_2}{\beta_1 + 2\beta_2 \log v_2 + \gamma_1 \log v_1}\right\} \tag{6.8}$$

Thus the isoquant will be negatively sloped if $v_1 > 1$, $v_2 > 1$ and $\alpha_1$, $\beta_1$, $\alpha_2$, $\beta_2$, $\gamma_1 > 0$, but in general the slope of the isoquant could be positive or negative.

Except in extreme circumstances the isoquant is also expected to be concave to the origin and this can be checked for any $(v_1, v_2)$ by evaluating the Hessian, if negative definite then the isoquants are concave to the origin *at that point*. The function is so flexible that each point of interest has to be separately evaluated.

## 6.4 Short-Run Product Curves for the Translog

In the short run it is assumed that one input (say $v_1$) is fixed. Thus the short-run production function has the form:

$$\log q = \log \beta_0 + \beta_1 \log v_2 + \beta_2 (\log v_2)^2 \tag{6.9}$$

(where $\beta_0$ is a constant).

Since $\log q$ can take any sign for positive values of q no restrictions can be placed on the coefficients.

The short-run *average* product of $v_2$ may be found by subtracting $\log v_2$ from both sides; thus:

$$\log\left(\frac{q}{v_2}\right) = \log \beta_0 + (\beta_1 - 1)\log v_2 + \beta_2 (\log v_2)^2 \tag{6.10}$$

To see how the average product changes with $v_2$ differentiate $(q/v_2)$ w.r.t. $v_2$ to yield

$$\frac{d\left(\dfrac{q}{v_2}\right)}{dv_2} = \frac{d\log}{dv_2}\left(\frac{q}{v_2}\right) = q\left[(\beta_2 - 1) + 2\beta_2 \log v_2\right]\cdot v_2^{-2} \qquad (6.11)$$

It is clear from (6.11) that the average product of $v_2$ will decrease with $v_2$ only if $\beta_1 + 2\beta_2 \log v_2 < 1$.

If $\beta_2$ is positive then increasing $v_2$ will eventually cause the average product of $v_2$ to *increase* with $v_2$.

The marginal product of $v_2$ is found by differentiating (6.9) w.r.t. $v_2$.

$$\text{MP}v_2 = \frac{\partial q}{\partial v_2} = \frac{q}{v_2}\left[\beta_1 + 2\beta_2 \log v_2\right] \qquad (6.12)$$

For the marginal product to be positive it is necessary that $(\beta_1 + 2\beta_2 \log v_2)$ is positive.

The law of diminishing returns requires the $MPv_2$ to diminish as $v_2$ increases. This law is therefore likely to be satisfied for only a small range of $v_2$. From this it follows that the translog function should not be taken to be a production function over the full range $0 < v < \infty$. It is, at best, a production function within a rather limited range of $v$. Unfortunately it is extremely difficult to express the legitimate range of $v$ in terms of the parameters of the function.

## 6.5 The Translog Cost Function

The translog cost function is not derived from any optimising procedure in the face of the translog production function. The translog has no self-dual.

The cost function is simply set up in the same way as the production function but in terms of costs and prices rather than in terms of quantities. Thus:

$$\begin{aligned}
\log C = {} & \log \delta_0 + \gamma_1 \log q + \alpha_1 \log P_1 + \beta_1 \log P_2 \\
& + \gamma_2 (\log q)^2 + \alpha_2 (\log P_1)^2 + \beta_2 (\log P_2)^2 \\
& + \delta_1 \log q \log P_1 + \delta_2 \log q \log P_2 \\
& + \delta_3 \log P_1 \log P_2
\end{aligned} \qquad (6.13)$$

This cost function must be restricted to be homogeneous of degree one in prices since doubling all prices and leaving all quantities unchanged must double costs.

To impose this restriction differentiate (6.13), thus:

$$\frac{dC}{C} = \alpha_1 \frac{dP_1}{P_1} + \beta_1 \frac{dP_2}{P_2} + \frac{2\alpha_2 \log P_1 \, dP_1}{P_1} + \frac{2\beta_2 \log P_2 \, dP_2}{P_1}$$

$$+ \frac{\delta_1 \log q \, dP_1}{P_1} + \frac{\delta_2 \log q \, dP_2}{P_2} + \frac{\delta_3 \log P_2 \, dP_1}{P_1}$$

$$+ \frac{\delta_3 \log P_1 \, dP_2}{P_2}$$

For equiproportionate changes in $P_1$ and $P_2$ say $dP/P$ we have:

$$\frac{dC}{C} \bigg/ \frac{dP}{P} = (\alpha_1 + \beta_1) + \log q(\delta_1 + \delta_2) + \log P_1(2\alpha_2 + \delta_3)$$

$$+ \log P_2(2\beta_2 + \delta_3)$$

Therefore constraining the cost function to be homogeneous of degree 1 in price requires:

$$(\alpha_1 + \beta_1) = 1$$

$$\delta_1 = -\delta_2$$

and

$$2\alpha_2 = 2\beta_2 = -\delta_3$$

Thus the translog cost function should be written as:

$$\log C = \log \delta_0 + \gamma_1 \log q + \log P_2 + \alpha_1 \log \left(\frac{P_1}{P_2}\right) + \gamma_2 (\log q)^2$$

$$+ \frac{\delta_3}{2}\left(\log \frac{P_1}{P_2}\right) + \delta_1 \log q \log \left(\frac{P_1}{P_2}\right) \qquad (6.14)$$

From this it is clear that doubling all prices would leave every term on the RHS unchanged except for $\log P_2$ which induces a doubling of $C$.

This cost function (6.14) is a translog in $q$ and $(P_1/P_2)$ (with the added $\log P_2$ term) rather than the unconstrained version (6.13) which is in terms of q, $P_1$ and $P_2$.

If this cost function is to be further constrained so that the underlying production function is assumed to have constant returns to scale then it is necessary that $\gamma_1 = 1$ and $\gamma_2 = 0 = \delta_1$. In which case (6.14) becomes:

$$\log\left(\frac{C}{q}\right) = \log \delta_0 + \log P_2 + \alpha_1 \log\left(\frac{P_1}{P_2}\right) + \frac{\delta_3}{2}\left(\log\frac{P_1}{P_2}\right)^2$$

## 6.6   The Elasticity of Substitution of the Translog

In Chapter 3 the elasticity of substitution was defined both in terms of $v_1$ and $v_2$ and in terms of the derivatives of the production function. The first is

$$\sigma = \frac{\mathrm{d}(v_1/v_2)}{(v_2/v_1)}\bigg/\frac{\mathrm{d}(\mathrm{d}v_2/\mathrm{d}v_1)}{(\mathrm{d}v_2/\mathrm{d}v_1)}$$

and the second is

$$\sigma = -\frac{f_1 f_2}{v_1 v_2}\, \varepsilon q \,/(f_{11}\cdot f_2^2 - 2f_1 f_2 \cdot f_{12} + f_{22}\cdot f_1^2) \tag{6.15}$$

when $\varepsilon$ are returns to scale. Using (6.15) yields for the translog:

$$\sigma = -\frac{\varepsilon}{q}\left\{A + B - 2\alpha_2\left(\frac{A}{B}\right) - 2\beta_2\left(\frac{B}{A}\right) - 2\gamma\right\}^{-1} \tag{6.16}$$

where   $A = \beta_1 + 2\beta_2 \log v_2 + \gamma_1 \log v_1$   and   $B = \alpha_1 + 2\alpha_2 \log v_1 + \gamma_1 \log v_2$. From (6.6) we have:

$$\varepsilon = A + B$$

Therefore

$$\sigma = -\frac{(A+B)}{q}\left\{A + B - 2\alpha_2\left(\frac{A}{B}\right) - 2\beta_2\left(\frac{B}{A}\right) - 2\gamma_1\right\}^{-1} \tag{6.17}$$

Thus the elasticity of substitution of the translog function depends on the level of output and on the level of $v_1$ and $v_2$.

## Appendix: Some Other Functional Forms

### *The Generalised Leontief Function*

This function is due to Diewert (1971) and he begins with a cost function of the form:

$$C = h(q)\sum_i \sum_j b_{ij} P_i \tag{A6.1}$$

which for our simple two-input case simplifies to:

$$C = h(q)(b_{11}P_1 + 2b_{12}P_1^{\frac{1}{2}}P_2^{\frac{1}{2}} + b_{22}P_2) \tag{A6.2}$$

We know from Shephard that $\partial C / \partial P_i = \hat{v}_i$ where $\hat{v}_1$ is the cost minimising level of input of $v_1$. Therefore

$$\frac{\partial C}{\partial P_i} = h(q)\left(b_{11} + b_{12}\left[\frac{P_2}{P_1}\right]^{\frac{1}{2}}\right) = \hat{v}_1$$

and $\qquad\qquad\qquad\qquad\qquad\qquad\qquad\qquad\qquad$ (A6.3)

$$\frac{\partial C}{\partial P_2} = h(q)\left(b_{22} + b_{12}\left[\frac{P_1}{P_2}\right]^{\frac{1}{2}}\right) = \hat{v}_2$$

(which are the factor demand equations). Using (A6.3) to eliminate $(P_1/P_2)$ we get:

$$\left[\frac{v_1}{h(q)} - b_{11}\right]\left[\frac{v_2}{h(q)} - b_{22}\right] = b_{12}^2 \tag{A6.4}$$

From this we can get some idea of the possible range of isoquants of the production function dual of (A6.2). Thus for instance when $b_{12} = 0$:

$$v_1 = h(q)b_{11} \quad \text{and} \quad v_2 = h(q)b_{22} \tag{A6.5}$$

which is the Leontief fixed coefficient case with rectangular isoquants.

When $b_{11}, b_{22}$ and $b_{12} > 0$ then as $[v_1/h(q)] \to 0$, $v_2 \to \infty$ and vice versa. Thus the unit isoquants are convex to the origin with asymptotes $b_{11}$ and $b_{22}$ for $v_1$ and $v_2$ respectively.

When $b_{11} < 0$, $b_{22}$ and $b_{12} > 0$ the asymptote of $v_1$ is a negative quantity and hence the isoquant will intersect the $v_2$ axis.

Finally, when $b_{11}$ and $b_{22} < 0$ and $b_{12} > 0$ the isoquants intersect both axes.

These four cases are shown in Figure A6.1.

## Returns to Scale and the Generalised Leontief Function

This can be found by totally differentiating the production function (equation (A6.4)) and then letting

$$\frac{\mathrm{d}v_1}{v_1} = \frac{\mathrm{d}v_2}{v_2} = \frac{1}{\varepsilon}\frac{\mathrm{d}q}{q} = \frac{\mathrm{d}v}{v}$$

**FIGURE A6.1**

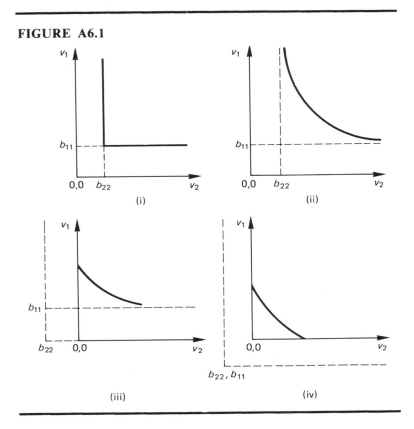

where $\varepsilon$ is returns to scale. Thus (A6.4) becomes:

$$\frac{v_1 v_2}{h^2(q)} - \frac{b_{22} v_1}{h(q)} - \frac{b_{11} v_2}{h(q)} = b_{12}^2 - b_{11} b_{12} \qquad \text{(A6.6)}$$

Thus:

$$0 = \frac{dv_1}{v_1} \frac{v_1 v_2}{h^2(q)} + \frac{dv_2}{v_2} \frac{v_1 v_2}{h^2(q)}$$

$$- \frac{2 v_1 v_2 h'(q) q \, dq}{h^3(q)} - \frac{b_{22} v_1}{h(q)} \frac{dv_1}{v_1} + \frac{b_{22} v_1 q h'(q)}{h^2(q)} \frac{dq}{q}$$

$$- \frac{b_{11} v_2}{h(q)} \frac{dv_2}{v_2} + \frac{b_{11} v_2 q h'(q)}{h^2(q)} \frac{dq}{q}$$

Therefore

$$\frac{dv}{v}\left[\frac{2v_1v_2}{h^2(q)} - \frac{b_{22}v_1}{h(q)} - \frac{b_{11}v_2}{h(q)}\right]$$

$$= \frac{dq}{q}\left[\frac{2v_2v_1h'(q)q}{h^3(q)} - \frac{b_{22}v_1h'(q)q}{h^2(q)} - \frac{b_{11}v_2h'(q)q}{h^2(q)}\right]$$

$$\varepsilon = \frac{dq}{q}\frac{v}{dv}$$

$$= \frac{h^{-1}(q)\left[\dfrac{2v_1v_2}{h(q)} - b_{22}v_1 - b_{11}v_2\right]}{\dfrac{h'(q)q}{h^2(q)}\left[\dfrac{2v_1v_2}{h(q)} - b_{22}v_1 - b_{11}v_2\right]} = \frac{h(q)}{h'(q)q} \tag{A6.7}$$

Thus for example if $h(q)$ is of the form $q^\alpha$ then returns to scale $= (1/\alpha)$. It is clear from (A6.7) that the returns to scale of the Generalised Leontief can be made a function of output ($q$). But the returns to scale do not vary along an isoquant (i.e. $\varepsilon$ is independent of $v_1/v_2$).

There are many generalisations of the standard production functions. One which includes most is suggested by Vazquez (1971) and takes the form:

$$q = A\left[bv_1^{-c(1+a)} + (1+a)\left(\frac{v_1}{v_2}\right)^{-ac}v_2^{-c(1+a)}\right]^{-\lambda/c(1+a)} \tag{A6.8}$$

This has returns to scale $\lambda$ and an elasticity of substitution:

$$\sigma = \frac{a + b(v_2/v_1)^c}{a + b(1+c)(v_2/v_1)^c}$$

Thus its returns to scale do not vary with scale or with factor proportions. Whereas the elasticity of substitution is independent of scale but varies with factor proportions. If $b = 0$ then (A6.8) becomes:

$$q = A\left[(1+a)^{-\lambda/c(1+a)}v_1^{\lambda a/1+a}v_2^{\lambda/1+a}\right]$$

and $\sigma = 1$ which is a Cobb–Douglas function of returns to scale $\lambda$. If $a = 0$ then (A6.8) becomes

$$q = A\left[bv_1^{-c} + v_2^{-c}\right]^{-\lambda/c}$$

and

$$\sigma = \frac{1}{1+c}$$

which is a CES function with returns to scale $\lambda$. If $C = -1$ then (A6.8) becomes:

$$q = A \left[ bv_1^{(1+a)} + (1+a) \left( \frac{v_1}{v_2} \right)^a v_2^{(1+a)} \right]^{1/1+a}$$

and

$$\sigma = 1 + \frac{b}{a} \left( \frac{v_1}{v_2} \right)$$

This function therefore relates the elasticity of substitution of $v_2$ for $v_1$ linearly to the ratio of $v_1/v_2$ hence it is called the Inverted Variable Elasticity of Substitution function (IVES) and is due to Zellner and Revankar (1969).

This Revankar function is homothetic since

$$\frac{dv_2}{dv_1} = - \left[ b + a \left( \frac{v_2}{v_1} \right) \right]$$

Hence the slope of the isoquant is the same along any ray from the origin (i.e. for any $[v_2/v_1]$). In this respect it is a Homothetic Isoquant Production Function (HIPF). This is a class of function suggested by Clemhout (1968). She suggested:

$$q = F(f(v_1, v_2))$$

where $f(v_1, v_2)$ is homogeneous of degree unity and $F$ determines the returns to scale.

The function $f(v_1, v_1)$ has the form

$$f(v_1, v_2) = v_2 e^{\int \phi(x) dx}$$

where

$$\phi(x) = \frac{1}{\left( \dfrac{v_1}{v_2} \right) - \left( \dfrac{dv_1}{dv_2} \right)}$$

The homotheticity requires that $(dv_1/dv_2) = \Omega(v_1/v_2)$. This function is therefore of the form:

$$q = F \left( v_2 e^{\int \phi(x) dx} \right)$$

where

$$\phi(x) = \frac{1}{\left[\dfrac{v_1}{v_2} - \Omega\left(\dfrac{v_1}{v_2}\right)\right]}$$

The elasticity of substitution of this function is:

$$\sigma = \frac{\Omega\left(\dfrac{v_1}{v_2}\right)}{\left(\dfrac{v_1}{v_2}\right)\Omega'\left(\dfrac{v_1}{v_2}\right)}$$

where

$$\Omega'\left(\frac{v_1}{v_2}\right) \text{ is } \frac{d\left[\Omega\left(\dfrac{v_1}{v_2}\right)\right]}{d\left(\dfrac{v_1}{v_2}\right)}$$

Thus the elasticity of substitution is a function only of the factor proportions.

If, for example $\dfrac{dv_1}{dv_2} = -\left[\dfrac{(1-\delta)}{\delta}\dfrac{v_1}{v_2}\right]^{1+e} = \Omega\left(\dfrac{v_1}{v_2}\right)$

then the HIPF reverts to the CES.

## Selected Reading

The Translog production function was first noted in L. R. Christensen, D. W. Jorgensen and L. J. Lau, 'Conjugate Duality and the Transcendental Logarithmic Production Function' (1971), *Econometrica*, July, pp. 255–6) and presented in full in L. R. Christensen, D. W. Jorgensen and L. J. Lau, 'Transcendental Logarithmic Production Frontiers', (1973), *Review of Economics and Statistics* (Feb.), pp. 28–45. Many empirical applications exist, one of the earliest being E. R. Berndt and D. O. Wood, 'Technology, Prices and the Derived Demand for Energy' (1975), *Review of Economics and Statistics*, LVII (3) Aug.

The Generalised Leontief function may be found in Diewert (1971). The very general function of Vasquez (1971) includes that of Clemhout (1968) and Zellner and Revankar (1969).

# Technological Progress

7

## 7.1 Introduction

A production function has been described above as the function relating inputs to outputs of production processes when all inputs are efficiently used. By 'efficiently' is meant that no more than is necessary of any input is used in the production of a given level of output.

The set of efficient production possibilities depends upon the laws of the physical sciences rather than those of the social sciences. As our knowledge and understanding of these laws extends and deepens so the set of efficient input combinations widens and new possibilities emerge. The production function therefore is not static.

## 7.2 Product Innovation and Process Innovation

Not only are new production processes discovered (process innovation) but new products also appear (product innovation).

This distinction (between process and production innovation) is useful but not always clear cut.

As a rule of thumb a process innovation could be confined to those innovations not apparent in the physical properties of the product, whereas product innovations require some adjustment on the part of the consumer.

In what follows, technological progress will be confined to *process* innovations – new ways of making things. Technological progress will therefore mean that the set of efficient input combinations available today will at least include, and partly dominate, the set of efficient input combinations available yesterday. In terms of isoquants, technological progress means that they move towards the origin as our knowledge grows.

## 7.3 Embodied and Disembodied Technological Progress

Capital may be assumed to be homogeneous such that any one piece of capital is exactly like any other and is equally well suited to any task: more capital simply means more of the same. If this really is a true picture of capital then technological progress must affect all existing processes. If, for example, a new way of making candles was discovered, then all existing candle makers would increase their 'sets of efficient' input combinations immediately, costlessly and equally. Technological progress of this kind is 'disembodied'. It makes use of existing labour and existing capital to produce more of the same product.

An alternative view is that new technological progress requires some adaptation of existing processes. Existing labour will be assumed to be costlessly adaptable but capital, having been constructed to perform particular operations simply cannot adapt. The introduction of new production processes must therefore be accompanied by the introduction of new capital: this technological progress is therefore 'embodied' in the capital stock.

The possibility of embodied technological change has two important consequences. First it means that the efficiency of production will depend not only on the current state of knowledge, but also upon the rate of investment in new machines. The latest set of efficient input combinations, though available to all, can only be had at a price – the cost of replacing existing capital stock with new. Those firms which do choose from the latest production possibility frontier are said to be using 'best-practice techniques'. Firms which bought their capital last year would be using slightly less efficient equipment and those which bought capital some years ago will be using (by current standards) rather inefficient equipment. Salter (1960) has shown that this range of efficiencies is very wide indeed and much could be gained, even if there were no further technological progress, simply by more and more firms investing in the best-practice equipment.

This leads to the second implication of embodiment. Since particular pieces of capital now embody particular techniques it is no longer possible to regard all capital as the same. Capital being no longer homogeneous it becomes necessary to index it in some relevant way. The obvious index is its date of installation since, presumably, it embodies the best practice of the year. This gives rise to the 'vintage' capital stock concept: capital inputs are disaggregated into vintages with older vintages having less efficient input combinations than newer vintages.

*Putty–Clay.* This idea of vintages of capital can be tightened still further if we assumed that the capital installed in year '$t$' is confined not only to the *range* of input combinations available in that year, but is confined to the *precise* factor combination actually chosen in that year. Thus it could be argued that capital is constructed so as to require a fixed amount of other inputs and produce a fixed amount of output. In any one year the entrepreneur chooses the best-practice combination of inputs from the current production possibility frontier and is thereafter stuck, not with the whole frontier, but with a particular point on it. Before the capital is installed he can choose any combination on the frontier (capital is 'putty'). After the capital is installed he is constrained to use one and only one set of inputs (capital is 'clay').

This putty/clay nature of capital would give rise to 'vintage' capital stocks even in the absence of technological progress since the characteristics of any one year's capital would depend not only on the production possibilities represented by the putty but also on the factor prices upon which the choice was based. Changing factor prices would therefore give rise to a capital stock with a vintage tail of characteristics.

## 7.4 Neutrality of Technological Progress

Economists' interest in technological progress springs not only from the improved efficiency made possible but also on the implications it has for factor demands and factor rewards. In other words will technological progress reduce the demand for labour rather more than it reduces the demand for capital (*ceteris paribus*) and will it increase wage earnings more than interest earnings or vice versa? That is will technological progress be 'biased' or 'neutral'? These are questions of some significance to social scientists and there have been a number of approaches to them.

There are three types of neutrality most commonly discussed and are due to Hicks, Harrod and Solow respectively.

## Hicks neutrality

Hicks neutrality is associated with that kind of technological progress which leaves factor ratios unchanged if factor prices remain constant. That is such that:

$$\frac{K}{L} = H_1 \left( \frac{P_K}{P_L} \right)$$

where $H_1$ is any function.

Furthermore since for cost minimisation at any level of output $P_K/P_L = dL/dK$ we have:

$$\frac{dL}{dK} = H_1^{-1} \left( \frac{K}{L} \right) \tag{7.1}$$

which expresses the Hicks neutrality condition in terms purely of the production function without reference to prices. Any movement of the isoquants which shifts them toward the origin and which preserves (7.1) will be Hicks neutral technological progress.

## Harrod neutrality

Harrod neutrality is that associated with the technological progress which leaves capital–output ratios unchanged if the price of capital (interest rate) is held constant.

$$\frac{K}{q} = H_2 (P_K)$$

where $H_2$ is any function.

Thus Harrod neutral technological progress implies that if $P_K$ is constant, then so is the capital–output ratio.

## Solow neutrality

The third, and final, type of neutrality is that due to Solow. Solow neutrality requires that if the wage rate remains unchanged then so will the labour–output ratio. Mathematically:

$$\frac{L}{q} = H_3(P_L)$$

## 7.5  Some Functional Forms

In order to explore these forms of neutrality further it is necessary to consider some particular functional forms of production function. Consider the Cobb–Douglas function:

$$q = AK^{\alpha}L^{\beta}$$

A common way of introducing technological progress into this function is to make '$A$' a function of time. This is tantamount to assuming that technological progress falls like manna from heaven: output increases (even when inputs are fixed) just because time passes.

If it is assumed, for example, that:

$$A = Be^{mt}$$

then

$$y = Be^{mt}K^{\alpha}L^{\beta}$$

and

$$\frac{\partial q}{\partial t} = mBe^{mt}K^{\alpha}L^{\beta} = mq$$

Hence

$$\frac{\partial q}{\partial t}\bigg/ q = m$$

Thus output grows at a constant proportionate rate of $m$ percent per year with no change in $L$ or $K$.

This new specification of the Cobb–Douglas yields

$$q = Be^{mt}K^{\alpha}L^{\beta}$$

Since

$$P_L = \frac{\partial q}{\partial L} = \frac{\beta q}{L} \quad \text{and} \quad \frac{\partial q}{\partial K} = \frac{\alpha q}{K} = P_k$$

we have

$$\frac{P_K}{P_L} = \frac{\alpha}{\beta} = \frac{L}{K}$$

Thus since $\alpha$ and $\beta$ are constants, there can be no change in factor rewards $[P_K/P_L]$ without any change in $[L/K]$. This means that the technological progress of this form, in this (Cobb–Douglas) function is Hicks neutral.

But it is also clear that the labour–output ratio will not change unless $P_L$ changes and that the capital–output ratio will not change unless $P_K$ changes. Thus this form of technological progress in the Cobb–Douglas function is also Harrod neutral and Solow neutral.

An alternative, and equally popular, way of specifying technological change is by way of *efficiency units*. This involves a respecification of the inputs $L$ and $K$. Whereas they are measured in man-hours and machine-hours respectively, it is hypothesised that as time passes each man hour becomes more 'efficient' and each capital hour becomes more 'efficient'. It is not therefore appropriate to put man-hours and machine-hours into the production function – what is needed is a measure of 'efficiency units'.

Let

$$K = e^{nt} K_a$$

and

$$L = e^{vt} L_a$$

where $K_a$ is actual capital hours and $K$ is capital input in efficiency units. Similarly for $L$. This means that as time passes $K$ and $L$ increase in efficiency units even though $K_a$ and $L_a$ may not change.

Using this specification in the Cobb–Douglas function yields:

$$q = A (e^{nt} K_a)^\alpha (e^{vt} L_a)^\beta$$

therefore

$$q = A e^{\alpha n t} e^{\beta v t} K_a{}^\alpha L_a{}^\beta$$

and

$$q = A e^{(\alpha n + \beta v)t} K_a{}^\alpha L_a{}^\beta$$

As can be seen this is identical to the previous form in which technological progress was introduced into the Cobb–Douglas function by way of changes in $A$.

This result does not, however, apply to all functional forms or all types of technological progress.

Consider next the CES function.

$$q^{-\theta} = \gamma^{-\theta}\delta K^{-\theta} + \gamma^{-\theta}(1-\delta)L^{-\theta}$$

The equivalent in this function to changing '$A$' in the Cobb–Douglas function is to change $\gamma$ – the CES efficiency parameter. Therefore let

$$\gamma = Be^{mt}$$

therefore

$$q^{-\theta} = (Be^{mt})^{-\theta}\delta K^{-\theta} + (Be^{mt})^{-\theta}(1-\delta)L^{-\theta}$$

and

$$\frac{\partial q}{\partial t}\bigg/ q = m$$

Thus, as in the case of the Cobb–Douglas, output grows at a constant proportionate rate $m$ per cent per year.

From the new specification of the CES we have:

$$P_K = \frac{\partial q}{\partial K} = Be^{-m\theta t}\delta\left(\frac{q}{K}\right)^{\theta+1}$$

$$P_L = \frac{\partial q}{\partial L} = Be^{-m\theta t}(1-\delta)\left(\frac{q}{L}\right)^{\theta+1}$$

Therefore

$$\frac{P_K}{P_L} = \frac{\delta}{(1-\delta)}\left(\frac{L}{K}\right)^{\theta+1}$$

From which it is clear that:

(a) This form of technological progress will cause $(q/K)$ to change even if $P_K$ is constant. It is not, therefore, Harrod neutral.
(b) This form of technical progress will cause $(q/L)$ to change even if $P_L$ is constant. It is not, therefore, Solow neutral.
(c) $L/K$ is constant when $(P_k/P_L)$ is constant. Therefore it is Hicks neutral.

In order to obtain a CES function with technological progress which is not Hicks neutral we could introduce the idea of efficiency units again. In this case the CES becomes:

$$y^{-\theta} = \gamma^{-\theta}\delta (e^{nt}K_a)^{-\theta} + \gamma^{-\theta}(1-\delta)(e^{vt}L_a)^{-\theta}$$

From which:

$$P_K = \frac{\partial q}{\partial K} = \gamma^{-\theta} \delta e^{-n\theta t} \left(\frac{q}{K}\right)^{\theta+1}$$

and

$$P_L = \frac{\partial q}{\partial L} = \gamma^{-\theta}(1-\delta) e^{-v\theta t} \left(\frac{q}{L}\right)^{\theta+1}$$

and:

$$\frac{P_K}{P_L} = \frac{\delta}{(1-\delta)} e^{(v-n)\theta t} \left(\frac{L}{K}\right)^{\theta+1}$$

Thus when technological progress is expressed in terms of efficiency units it will not necessarily be Hicks neutral. (*Note*: it can of course be rendered Hicks neutral if $v = n$.) It collapses to the Harrod neutral case when $n = 0$ and to the Solow neutral case when $v = 0$.

Thus, for the CES function, technological change will be Hicks neutral when actual labour improves (is augmented) at the same rate as actual capital improves (is augmented) – $(n = v)$. Because both factors are being augmented at the same rate, this is called 'product' or 'output' augmenting technological progress.

The CES will have Harrod neutral technological progress when only labour augmentation occurs $(n = 0, v \neq 0)$. Harrod neutrality is therefore *labour augmenting* technological progress.

Finally, the CES will have Solow neutral technological progress when only capital augmentation occurs $(n \neq 0, v = 0)$. Solow neutrality is therefore *capital augmenting* technological progress.

Finally, consider the *translog function*. The translog function has the form:

$$\log q = \log \gamma_0 + \alpha_1 \log L + \beta_1 \log K + \alpha_2 (\log L)^2 + \beta_2 (\log K)^2$$
$$+ \gamma_1 \log L \log K$$

and one possible way of introducing technological progress would be by way of the first term, that is let $\gamma_0 = \gamma_0 e^{mt}$. Thus

$$\log y_t = \log \gamma_0 + \log e^{mt} + \alpha_1 \log L + \beta_1 \log K + \alpha_2 (\log L)^2$$
$$+ \beta_2 (\log L)^2 + \gamma_1 \log L \log K$$

From which, if $L$ and $K$ remains constant, $\log q_t = m \cdot t + \log q_0$ where $q_0$ is the output at time 0. Differentiating w.r.t. time we have:

$$\frac{dq_t}{dt} \cdot \frac{1}{q} = m$$

Thus $q$ grows at a constant proportionate rate $m$ percent per year. From Chapter 6 we have that

$$P_L = \frac{dq}{dL} = \frac{q}{L}(\alpha_1 + 2\alpha_2 \log L + \gamma_1 \log K) \tag{7.2}$$

$$P_K = \frac{dq}{dK} = \frac{q}{K}(\beta_1 + 2\beta_2 \log K + \gamma_1 \log L) \tag{7.3}$$

hence

$$\frac{P_L}{P_K} = \frac{K}{L}\left\{\frac{\alpha_1 + 2\alpha_2 \log L + \gamma_1 \log K}{\beta_1 + 2\beta_2 \log K + \gamma_1 \log L}\right\} \tag{7.4}$$

Since, with technological progress, $q$ grows over time it is clear from (7.2) and (7.3) that this form of TP is neither Harrod nor Solow neutral. It could, however, be Hicks neutral if the term in the curly brackets of (7.4) were constant. This is the case under constant returns to scale since then

$$\alpha_1 + \beta_1 = 1, \, 2\alpha_2 = -\gamma_1$$

and

$$2\beta_2 = -\gamma_1.$$

Thus

$$\frac{P_L}{P_K} = \frac{K}{L}\left\{\frac{1 - \beta_1 - \gamma_1 \log L + \gamma_1 \log K}{\beta_1 - \gamma_1 \log K + \gamma_1 \log L}\right\}$$

that is

$$\frac{P_L}{P_K} = \frac{K}{L}\left\{\frac{1 - \beta_1 + \gamma_1 \log(K/L)}{\beta_1 - \gamma_1 \log(K/L)}\right\}$$

which yields constant $K/L$ when $PL/PK$ is constant.

Hence the CRTS translog has Hicks neutral technological progress when $\gamma_0$ becomes an increasing function of time.

The alternative way of introducing technological progress would be by way of efficiency units. In this case let $L_t = e^{nt}L_0$ and $K_t = e^{mt}K_0$. Thence

$$\text{Log } q_t = \gamma_0 + \alpha_1 \log L_0 + \alpha_1 mt + \beta_1 \log K_0 + \beta_1 nt$$
$$+ \alpha_2 (\log L_0 + mt)^2$$
$$+ \beta_2 (\log K_0) + nt)^2 + \gamma_1 (\log L_0 + mt)(\log K_0 + nt)$$

$$\text{Log } q_t = \text{Log } q_0 + (n\alpha_1 + \beta_1 n)t + (2\alpha_2 m + \gamma_1 n)t \log L_0$$
$$+ (2\beta_2 n + \gamma_1 m)t \log K_0 + (m^2\alpha_2 + n^2\beta_2 + \gamma_1 nm)t^2$$

This is a rather complicated expression but if we have CRTS and $n = m = \rho$ then

$$\text{Log } q_t = \log q_0 \, e^{\rho t}$$

Therefore

$$\frac{\partial q_t}{dt} \cdot \frac{1}{y_t} = \rho$$

which is identical with the case where $\gamma_0 = \gamma e^{nt}$.

## 7.6 Learning by Doing

The assumption that technological progress is a function of time, though widely used, is not without its critics. Quite why the passage of time should of itself improve productivity is very difficult to explain and thus time must be a proxy for something which actually does explain technological progress.

It is a weak proxy in that typically factor inputs have been growing over time and hence the scale of operations is highly correlated with time. It therefore becomes very difficult empirically to distinguish between technological progress and returns to scale. The sharp reductions in the output of some sectors in the recent past may help resolve some of these econometric problems.

One explanation of technological progress (offered by Arrow, 1962) is that as producers gain experience at producing something they become more and more efficient at it. Labour finds new ways of doing things so that relatively minor modifications to plant and procedures can contribute to higher and higher levels of productivity. This argument has a certain appeal and suggests that cumulative output (as a measure of 'experience') rather than a time trend, should act as a proxy for technological progress. In the case where the process remains the same 'size', learning by doing is indistinguishable from the exponential time trend since

$$q_1 = q_0 + nq_0 = (n+1)q_0$$
$$q_2 = q_1 + nq_1 = (n+1)q_1 = (n+1)^2 q_0$$

etc.

Where $q_0$ is the output in period '0' with a given amount of capital and labour. In the next period, with exactly the same amount of capital and labour, the plant has 'learned' to produce $n$ per cent more simply because it has 'experienced' producing $q_0$. In period 2 the same amount of capital and labour will produce $q_1$ plus an additional $n$ per cent due to the experience of having produced $q_1$ in the past. Eventually we get:

$$q_T = (n+1)^T q_0$$

where $q_T$ is output at time period $T$, $n$ is the learning factor (a constant) and $q_0$ is output in period '0'.

Thus in this case, where labour and capital are constant, output grows with time and hence time is as good a proxy for technological progress as is cumulative output.

Of course the learning by doing is not necessarily constrained in this way since factor inputs could change over time and the simple exponential path would be discarded.

It is therefore more general than the time trend and is better supported than simply assuming that efficiency grows with time.

The fact that efficiency gains are associated with output rather than time does not of course mean that they are the same as returns to scale. They are distinct in that they depend upon *cumulative* rather than *current* output and are not lost when output levels fall – once producers have learned how to produce more efficiently they can do so whatever level of current output. If these efficiency gains had been achieved merely by the scale of production then they would be lost should the scale of production fall back to its original level.


## 7.7   Research and Development

Technological progress may be, at least partially, explained by learning by doing but there is a rather more purposeful way of learning how and what to produce. This 'directed' pursuit of know-how falls under the heading of Research and Development. Firms, or groups of firms, devote some labour and some capital, not to producing current output, but rather to actively seek out new products and new processes. These labour and capital inputs into the pursuit of knowledge would seem to be an obvious proxy for their 'output', that is new knowledge.

The difficulty with this is that unlike the known production function for products there is no well specified production function for knowledge. Some firms may devote quite large sums to Research and Development and yet never actually come up with any new product or process. Other firms may spend a small sum on R & D and stumble on some new product or process which pays an immense rate of return on the original R & D outlay. It is well known that R & D is a very uncertain activity and it is not clear that entrepreneurs can make rational choices about how much to spend on it.

In some cases, the new knowledge immediately becomes public knowledge and hence available to all the firms in the industry rather than just the firm which made the original investment. This has led some (Galbraith, 1952; Schumpeter, 1947) to argue that only very large firms would engage in R & D since, by being large they will receive the bulk of the profits from any new knowledge. There is some evidence (Mansfield, 1969) that large firms do invest more in R & D than do little firms but not more than do medium size firms. There seems then to be a threshold below which firms do no R & D and above which firms do R & D.

If, as has been supposed, R & D does 'produce' knowledge then productivity should in some positive way be correlated to R & D expenditure. The cross-sectional evidence on a national level does not support this view. The decline in some countries relative to others is not highly correlated with their respective R & D expenditures. There is, however, some evidence to support this view when applied across industries. Those industries which spend a lot on R & D tend to have higher productivity growth than those which spend little. There is some a priori support for this view too since it is very unlikely that profit seeking entrepreneurs would continue to spend large sums on R & D unless they occasionally experienced some successes.

It cannot be inferred from this that increasing R & D would necessarily increase productivity. Those industries which tend not to spend on R & D may be correct in believing that such expenditure is a waste. Persuading them to increase their R & D expenditure will therefore not result in increased productivity.

## 7.8 Patents

Since R & D adds to our stock of knowledge and since it is the stock of knowledge which enters the production function it is necessary to find some appropriately weighted sum of past expenditures as an argument in the production function (Schott, 1976).

A rather more direct way of measuring the new knowledge flowing from R & D is not just to measure expenditures (some of which is wasted) but to measure the actual successes. This can be done since many of the successful results of R & D are patented. Thus some idea of the 'output' of new knowledge can be gained by collecting data on new patents. In order to classify and aggregate patents it is necessary to have some idea of the physical process or product under review.

This moves the investigation away from the variables economists know about back to engineering concepts.

It is nevertheless a promising way forward.

## 7.9   Technological Progress and Economic Growth

Growth processes can be studied both from the micro and from the macro aspect. The macro studies dominate the literature but the concepts and definitions also apply to the micro level. But let us for simplicity assume that we want to analyse the growth process in a whole economy, and that we have a macro production function:

$$Q = F(K, L) \tag{7.5}$$

We then assume that inputs and outputs change over time and also that technological progress alters the form of the production function over time. Output at time '$t$' is therefore a function of the inputs at time '$t$' ($K(t)$ and $L(t)$ and time itself ($t$)). Hence:

$$Q(t) = F(K(t), L(t), t) \tag{7.6}$$

Taking the total derivative of this function yields:

$$dQ = F_K dK + F_L dL + F_t dt \tag{7.7}$$

where

$$F_k = \frac{\partial Q}{\partial K}, \quad F_L = \frac{\partial Q}{\partial L} \quad \text{and} \quad F_t = \frac{\partial Q}{\partial t}$$

Total growth of output ($dQ$) therefore has three sources; growth of capital $dK$, growth of labour $dL$ and technological progress $dt$. The interpretation of the last term is very straightforward if we observe that $F_t \mathrm{d}t$ equals growth of total ouput with capital and labour remaining constant. ($\mathrm{d}K = \mathrm{d}L = 0$). It is accordingly very natural to interpret $F_t \mathrm{d}t$ as the part of total growth resulting from technical progress.

The formula (7.7) can be used to identify the different sources to growth. But it can also be used for a more direct study of technological progress. If we knew $\mathrm{d}Q$, $F_K \mathrm{d}K$ and $F_L \mathrm{d}L$, we could simply calculate the 'technological progress term' as the remainder term, that is $F_t \mathrm{d}t = \mathrm{d}Q - F_K \mathrm{d}K - F_L \mathrm{d}L$. This calculation can in fact be done *even though we know nothing of the form of the production function F*.

To see this, consider equation (7.7)

$$\mathrm{d}Q = F_K \mathrm{d}K + F_L \mathrm{d}L + F_t \mathrm{d}t$$

Therefore

$$\frac{\mathrm{d}Q}{\mathrm{d}t} \frac{1}{Q} = \frac{F_K \cdot K}{Q} \cdot \frac{\mathrm{d}K}{\mathrm{d}t} \cdot \frac{1}{K} + \frac{F_L \cdot L}{Q} \cdot \frac{\mathrm{d}L}{\mathrm{d}t} \frac{1}{L} + \frac{F_t}{Q} \qquad (7.8)$$

But from our first order conditions we have that:

$$F_K = P_K \quad \text{and} \quad F_L = P_L$$

also we have that:

$$\frac{\mathrm{d}Q}{\mathrm{d}t} \frac{1}{Q} = \dot{Q}, \frac{\mathrm{d}K}{\mathrm{d}t} \frac{1}{K} = \dot{K} \quad \text{and} \quad \frac{\mathrm{d}L}{\mathrm{d}t} \frac{1}{L} = \dot{L}$$

Therefore

$$\dot{Q} = \frac{P_K K}{Q} \cdot \dot{K} + \frac{P_L L}{Q} \cdot \dot{L} + \frac{Ft}{Q} \qquad (7.9)$$

But $P_K K/Q$ is capital's share in output, $S_K$, and $P_L L/Q$ is labour's share in output, $S_L$.
Hence:

$$\dot{Q} = S_K \dot{K} + S_L \dot{L} + \frac{F_t}{Q} \qquad (7.10)$$

Therefore if we know changes in output ($\dot{Q}$), changes in capital ($\dot{K}$), changes in labour ($\dot{L}$) and the factor shares in national income ($S_K$ and

$S_L$) we can find $F_t/Q$, that is by how much output would change if only time changed and capital and labour were constant.

$$F_t/Q = \dot{Q} - S_K \cdot \dot{K} - S_L \cdot \dot{L}$$

Thus, we can calculate the rate of technological progress without knowing the form of the macro production function. Consider for instance the following Swedish data:

| Period | Rate of growth of capital | Rate of growth of labour | Capital income share | Labour income share |
|---|---|---|---|---|
| 1950–60 | 0.451 | 0 | 0.36 | 0.64 |
| 1961–70 | 0.486 | 0 | 0.35 | 0.65 |
| 1971–80 | 0.425 | −0.02 | 0.33 | 0.67 |

The figures refer to the whole decade. They furthermore refer to the whole of the Swedish economy.

The growth of GNP was 39.1 per cent between 1951–60, 53.9 per cent 1961–70 and 21.0 per cent 1971–80. Inserting these figures into our equation (7.12) yields:

| Period | Growth resulting from increased capitail (%) | Growth resulting from increased labour (%) | Growth from technical progress (%) |
|---|---|---|---|
| 1951–60 | 15.7 | 0 | 23.4 |
| 1961–70 | 17.0 | 0 | 36.9 |
| 1971–1980 | 14.9 | −1.3 | 7.4 |

We notice here a dramatic change in technical progress. GNP increased 36.9 per cent during the 1960s due to technical progress, while that figure was only 7.4 per cent during the 1970s. Of course one can go further and ask for the reasons for this changing rate of technical progress. But our purpose here was only to demonstrate the simplicity of the analysis and the potential usefulness of the production function concept.

## 7.10  Summary and Conclusions

This chapter deals with some of the principal issues which are raised for production functions by the existence of technical progress. To a large extent this is a matter for engineer and scientist whose function it is to know the physical laws which govern production possibilities. Economists do, however, have a great interest in this question and have tried to address it by finding suitable proxies for changes in knowledge and by classifying such changes according to whether they are:

(a) Embodied or disembodied.
(b) Hicks neutral, Harrod netural or Solow neutral.

The usual proxy for technological knowledge is time itself but this is not well founded in theory. Learning by doing is intuitively appealing and has some well documented support.

The existence of Research and Development departments suggests that some technological progress has been sought and found outside the actual process of producing commodities. Expenditure on R & D may therefore provide a better proxy for technological change than time or cumulated output alone. This may be refined by focusing on only successful R & D by using statistics on patents rather than total R & D expenditure. What is not clear is whether R & D seeks a direction of change as well as the pace of change.

Finally, the idea of technological progress is investigated as an element in the growth of output of the Swedish economy. It turns out that quite simple and rather elegant results can be obtained.

For a comprehensive bibliography of the literature on technological progress see Stubbs and Metcalfe (1980) and for a survey see Kennedy and Thirlwall (1972).

# From Firms to Industry: the Johansen Production Model

## 8.1 Introduction

As defined above, the production function refers to the micro decision making unit: for example the 'firm' or the 'plant'. However, economists often use the notion of a production function to describe relationships between aggregates of some kind. These 'aggregate production functions' may refer to an 'industry' or a 'sector' or even to the whole economy and purport to represent the range of possible inputs of aggregate labour, and aggregate capital etc. capable of producing various levels of aggregate output.

The existence of such aggregate relationships has been widely questioned and the difficulties of aggregating micro production functions into such aggregates impose very strong restrictions on the forms of function admissible.

In this chapter it is demonstrated how an aggregate function can be derived from a number of micro functions in a consistent manner. The 'aggregate' considered here is the 'industry' level where firms are aggregated according to their standard industrial classfication (SIC) (say at the two digit level), such that they are regarded as producing one homogeneous, physically measurable output.

The presentation here derives from the Leif Johansen production model, presented in full in Johansen (1972). The most important element in this model is the distinction between *ex ante* and *ex post* concepts which correspond to our long and short run. Some important pieces of Johansen's model have already been presented at various places in this book: for example the distinction between substitution possibilities before and after the investment, the different role of capital before and after an investment and the difference between a firm and an industry cost curve. The Johansen production model unites all these pieces into an integrated model with long- and short-run micro and aggregate production functions.

## 8.2 *Ex Ante* Functions at Micro and Industry Levels

Let the *ex ante* micro relation be:

$$q = f(K, L, E) \tag{8.1}$$

where $q$ is a single homogeneous output, $K$ is capital, $L$ is labour and $E$ is energy.

Assume that (8.1) exhibits constant returns to scale *at one, and only one*, level of output ($q^*$). Since we have CRTS we can divide through by $q^*$ to yield

$$1 = f(\xi_K, \xi_L, \xi_E) \tag{8.2}$$

where $\xi_i$ is the input–output coefficient of factor $i$, that is the amount of factor $i$ required to produce one unit of output is called the *techniques relation* in Johansen's terminology. It is the 'frontier' in the input coefficient space: it is not possible to produce with lower input coefficient combinations. To illustrate this idea further consider the micro function:

$$\log q = \log A - K^{-\alpha_1} L^{-\alpha_2} E^{-\alpha_3} \tag{8.3}$$

Taking the differential gives

$$\frac{dq}{q} = \frac{\alpha_1 K^{-\alpha_1} L^{-\alpha_2} E^{-\alpha_3}}{K} dK + \frac{\alpha_2 K^{-\alpha_1} L^{-\alpha_2} E^{-\alpha_3}}{L} dL$$

$$+ \frac{\alpha_3 K^{-\alpha_1} L^{-\alpha_2} E^{-\alpha_3}}{E} dE$$

For returns to scale we have

$$\frac{dK}{K} = \frac{dL}{L} = \frac{dE}{E} = \frac{dF}{F}$$

$$\frac{dq}{q} = \frac{dF}{F} (K^{-\alpha} L^{-\alpha_2} E^{-\alpha_3}) (\alpha_1 + \alpha_2 + \alpha_3)$$

Therefore

$$\text{RTS} = \frac{\mathrm{d}q}{q} \Big/ \frac{\mathrm{d}F}{F} = (\log A - \log q^*)(\alpha_1 + \alpha_2 + \alpha_3)$$

Thus for CRTS $(\mathrm{d}q/q)/(\mathrm{d}F/F) = 1$ and:

$$1 = (\log A - \log q^*)(\alpha_1 + \alpha_2 + \alpha_3) \tag{8.4}$$

which yields $(q^*)$: the unique level of output at which (8.3) exhibits CRTS.

At this scale of output we have $q = q^*$, $K^* = \xi_k . q^*$, $L^* = \xi_L . q^*$ and $E^* = \xi_E . q^*$. Putting these values in (8.3) we get:

$$\log \hat{q} = \log A - (\xi_k \hat{q})^{-\alpha_1} . (\xi_L . \hat{q})^{-\alpha_2} . (\xi_E . \hat{q})^{-\alpha_3}$$
$$\log \hat{q} = \log A - \hat{q}^{-(\alpha_1 + \alpha_2 + \alpha_3)}(\xi_k)^{-\alpha_1} . (\xi_L)^{-\alpha_2} . (\xi_E)^{-\alpha_3}$$

Therefore

$$1 = (\log A - \log \hat{q})^{-1} \hat{q}^{-(\alpha_1 + \alpha_2 + \alpha_3)} [\xi_k^{-\alpha_1} . \xi_L^{-\alpha_2} . \xi_E^{-\alpha_3}]$$

But $(\log A - \log \hat{q})^{-1} \hat{q}^{-(\alpha_1 + \alpha_2 + \alpha_3)}$ is constant and may be set equal to '$B$'. Therefore

$$1 = B(\xi_K^{-\alpha_1} . \xi_L^{-\alpha_2} . \xi_E^{-\alpha_3}) \tag{8.5}$$

which is the 'technique relation' (in the sense of Johansen) derived from micro function (8.3).

The long-run industry function comprises points in the $\xi_K, \xi_L, \xi_E E$ space such as (8.5) since in the long run only firms of optimal scale are built. Thus if the industry produces $Q$ units of output using $V_K$ units of capital, $V_L$ units of labour and $V_E$ units of energy then (8.5) yields:

$$1 = B\left\{\left(\frac{V_K}{Q}\right)^{-\alpha_1}\left(\frac{V_L}{Q}\right)^{-\alpha_2}\left(\frac{V_E}{Q}\right)^{-\alpha_3}\right\}$$
$$Q^{-(\alpha_1 + \alpha_2 + \alpha_3)} = B(V_K)^{-\alpha_1}(V_L)^{-\alpha_2}(V_E)^{-\alpha_3}$$

Therefore

$$Q = B^\theta V_K^{\theta_1} V_L^{\theta_2} V_E^{\theta_3} \tag{8.6}$$

where $\theta = \dfrac{-1}{\alpha_1 + \alpha_2 + \alpha_3}$

$\theta_1 = \dfrac{\alpha_1}{\alpha_1 + \alpha_2 + \alpha_3}$

$\theta_2 = \dfrac{\alpha_2}{\alpha_1 + \alpha_2 + \alpha_3}$

$\theta_3 = \dfrac{\alpha_3}{\alpha_1 + \alpha_2 + \alpha_3}$

(8.6) is the long run, or *ex ante* industry function resulting from the aggregation of micro functions of form (8.3) when all micro units are built in the same optimal scale. *Note*: the aggregate function (8.6) exhibits constant returns to scale.

## 8.3 The *Ex Post* Micro Function

The short-run (or *ex post*) micro production function is characterised by two important technological conditions:

(i) Labour and energy are variable inputs but must be used in fixed proportions to output;
(ii) The amount of capital available is predetermined and hence each plant has an upper 'capacity' level of output.

The short-run micro production function for firm $i$ corresponding to the long-run micro production function (8.1) is accordingly fully characterised by:

$\xi_L^i$, the input coefficient for labour
$\xi_E^i$, the input coefficient for energy
$\bar{q}^i$, capacity output.

The production of firm $i$ must lie between zero and capacity, that is:

$$0 \leqslant q^i \leqslant \bar{q}^i \tag{8.7}$$

And its use of inputs is described by:

$$L^i = q^i \xi_L^i \tag{8.8}$$
$$E^i = q^i \xi_E^i$$

Equations (8.7) and (8.8) may also be expressed using the usual notation for the Leontief production function:

$$q^i = \text{Min}\,(L^i/\xi_L^i, E^i/\xi_E^i) \tag{8.9}$$

$$q^i \leqslant \bar{q}^i$$

## 8.4 The *Ex Post* Industry Production Function

The short-run industry (*ex post* macro, in Johansen's terminology) function is derived from the short-run firm functions. Let us assume that we have $N$ different firms (or plants) identified by the index '$i$'. Each firm has a production technology according to (8.9).

An industry production function is defined as the relation between the aggregates of inputs and output in an industry such that the maximum of output is obtained (given an industrial structure) from a given set of inputs. If we assume that aggregate inputs are $V_L$ and $V_E$, we therefore seek the solution to the problem:

$$\text{Max}\,Q = q_1 + q_2 + , \ldots , + q_N$$

Subject to:

$$V_L \geqslant \sum_i q^i \xi_L^i \tag{8.10}$$

$$V_E \geqslant \sum_i q^i \xi_E^i$$

$$0 \leqslant q^i \leqslant \bar{q}^i \qquad i = 1, \ldots , N$$

Equation (8.10) is an ordinary linear-programming problem and easy to solve with existing computer programs. For each value of $V_L$ and $V_E$ we will obtain a value of $Q$. The totality of all $V$'s and $Q$'s forms a relation:

$$Q = F\,(V_L; V_E) \tag{8.11}$$

which is the short-run industry function.

Each value of $V_L$ and $V_E$ coincides not only with a specific value of $Q$, but also with specific values of $q^i, i = 1, \ldots , N$ that is production in each plant. Each set of aggregate inputs corresponds therefore to a specific *distribution* of total production among the individual firms. Solving (8.10) is therefore the same thing as choosing a distribution among plants and it is to this choice that we turn next.

## 8.5 Competitive Markets and the Bang-Bang Solution

It is a firmly established result in economic theory that a competitive market is efficient in the sense that it ensures the best use of existing resources. In the field of production this implies that firms in a competitive market (and with a behaviour that corresponds to a competitive market) produce *on* the firm production functions. Furthermore, we know that each firm produces a quantity determined by the condition $MC^i = P$.

The result for single firms applies also to the industry level. In a competitive market we know that observed relation between aggregates of inputs and outputs is a point on the industry production function defined by (8.10). The solution to (8.10) can therefore be studied through the market solution.

We assume now that prices of inputs are fixed ($P_L$ and $P_E$) and that product price equals $P$. Firm $i$ has, according to our assumptions, a fixed input technology with input coefficients $\xi_L^i$ and $\xi_E^i$. Accordingly, it has a constant marginal cost curve:

$$MC^i = P_L \cdot \xi_L^i + P_E \cdot \xi_E^i \tag{8.12}$$

which holds up to $q = \bar{q}^i$. After that the marginal cost curve becomes vertical. (It also follows from the fixed input coefficients that marginal cost equals average variable cost for each firm.)

The market solution for firm $i$ is illustrated in Figure 8.1.

The 'Bang-Bang' character of the market solution is easily seen from Figure 8.1. If market price is higher than marginal (and average variable) cost, the firm will produce at full capacity. It will continue to do so until market price goes below the critical level $MC^i$. When that occurs, production will stop completely. When price is exactly equal to marginal cost $MC^i$, we have an indeterminate case (of which we shall say no more). In general, production in a firm will be either zero or at the full capacity point.

Now let us consider the market solution from the industry level. We assume that the firms, having chosen their plants at different times in the past, will have different input coefficients. This may be due to technical progress or to price changes. (Recall that before the plant is installed the entrepreneur has a choice of input coefficients and a choice of plant size (capacity). These choices will depend upon relative prices and his expectations of them. Thus as time passes, prices

---

**FIGURE 8.1**

**Illustration to the 'Bang-Bang' Solution of a Competitive Market**

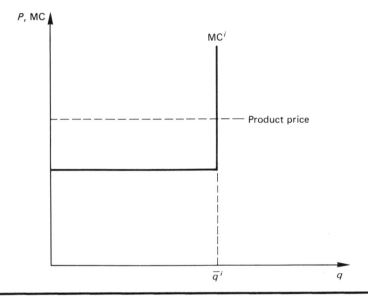

---

change, the choices of entrepreneurs will change and there will be a range of input coefficients.)

Such a range of input coefficients is shown in Figure 8.2. Firm 1 for example uses more of both labour and energy than does firm 2, per unit of output. Firm 3, however, uses more labour but less energy per unit of output than does firm 2.

In Figure 8.2 we have also indicated the straight line

$$P = P_L \xi_L + P_E \xi_E$$

If a firm i has input coefficients which lie on this line, that is if

$$P = P_L \xi_L^i + P_E \xi_E^i$$

the price will exactly cover average variable cost and it will earn zero quasi-rent on their fixed input (capital).

Any firm with coefficients to the south-west of the zero quasi-rent line will earn positive quasi-rents by operating and hence will be at full

**FIGURE 8.2**

**Input Coefficients (Crosses) and Quasi-rent Line of an Industry**

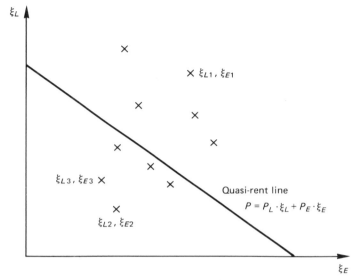

production. Any firm with coefficients to the north east of the zero quasi-rent line will make losses (earn negative quasi-rents) and hence be completely shut down.

This is the bang-bang solution as before with firms operating either at full capacity or not at all. The zero quasi-rent line is the line dividing firms into 'on' or 'off' firms.

## 8.6  The Short-run Industry Function Obtained Through A Competitive Market

Figure 8.2 can now be used to illustrate the construction of a short-run industry production function. We will first study the relation between industry inputs and outputs for given input prices (say for example those corresponding to the slope of the zero quasi-rent line in Figure 8.2).

If the product price ($P$) is reduced then the zero quasi-rent moves parallel to itself toward the origin. Thus more plants are switched off since they now lie north-east of the new zero quasi-rent line. Price could be reduced so low that no firms produce (zero industry output) or price could be raised so high that all firms are operating (capacity industry output).

Industry output will therefore grow from zero to maximum as the price rises and moves the zero quasi-rent line north-easterly. This trace of industry output against industry price is the 'expansion path'.

This expansion path will depend upon the chosen input prices. If relative input prices are changed then the zero quasi-rent line rotates and switches some plants 'on' and turns other plants off. By tracing out the expansion paths for every input price ratio it is possible to trace out all possible input–output combinations at an industry level.

In practice, of course, we need not consider all possible input price ratios. There will be a finite number of plants (points in the $\xi_L$, $\xi_E$ space) and only those relative price changes which switch these plants on or off are of interest.

In fact all these computations can be handled by computer programs.

## 8.7    Construction of an Isoquant – an Example

The construction of an isoquant of a short-run industry function can be illustrated with an empirical example. Let us assume that we have an industry with three firms. Input coefficients and capacity for these are given in Table 8.1. The input coefficients are displayed in Figure 8.3.

**TABLE 8.1**
**Characteristics of a Hypothetical Industry**

| Firm no. | $\xi_L$ | $\xi_E$ | Capacity |
|----------|---------|---------|----------|
| 1        | 1.0     | 1.0     | 100      |
| 2        | 2.0     | 1.2     | 150      |
| 3        | 1.3     | 2.0     | 200      |

## FIGURE 8.3
### Input Coefficients and Two Quasi-rent Lines

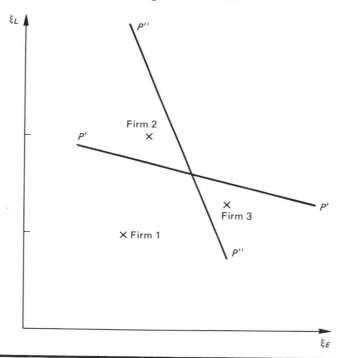

Let us now assume that we want to construct the isoquant for
$Q = 150$. It is easily seen from Figure 8.3 that firm 1 will *always*
produce at lower cost than the others, no matter what prices. We can
turn the quasi-rent line anyway we want, but firm 1 will always be the
first one to land on the SW side when the line moves outwards from
the origin. Thus we conclude that the 'first' 100 units will always be
produced by firm 1. What about the remaining 50? We see from
Figure 8.3 that whether firm 2 or firm 3 produces them depends on
the slope of the quasi-rent line ( = the ratio of input prices). If this line
has a slope parallel to P'P' (which indicates that factor $L$ is rather
expensive) it is obvious that firm 3 will produce the required extra 50
tons. If, on the other hand, the line is parallel to P"P", it is equally

obvious that firm 3 can produce at lowest cost. Thus we have the following alternatives open to us.

*Production of* 150 *units*

| *The first* 100 | *The remaining* 50 |
|---|---|
| Always firm 1 | Firm 2 *or* firm 3 |

If we assume that firm $i$ has input coefficient $\xi^i_L$ and $\xi^i_E$, we obtain the following aggregate factor demands:

*Factor consumption at* 150 *units*

| | | *The first* 100 *units* | | *The remaining* 50 |
|---|---|---|---|---|
| (1) *Labour* | either: | $100. \, \xi^1_L$ | $+$ | $50. \, \xi^2_L = V^1_L$ |
| | or: | $100. \, \xi^1_L$ | $+$ | $50. \, \xi^3_L = V^2_L$ |
| (2) *Energy* | either: | $100. \, \xi^1_E$ | $+$ | $50. \, \xi^2_E = V^1_E$ |
| | or: | $100. \, \xi^1_E$ | $+$ | $50. \, \xi^3_E = V^2_E$ |

These two points $(V^2_L V^2_E)$, $(V^3_L, V^3_E)$ are marked in Figure 8.4. Since we can produce the 50 units required in excess of firm 1's production with any *combination* of firms 2 and 3, it is apparent that total

**FIGURE 8.4**
**The Short-run Isoquant for 150 units (see text)**

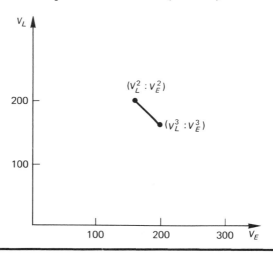

production possibilities for the level $Q = 150$ are given by the straight line between the two points in Figure 8.4, that is any convex combination of $(V_L^2, V_E^2)$ and $(V_L^3, V_E^3)$. This being the whole set of labour and energy inputs capable of producing 150 units of output it must be the *isoquant* for 150.

This being the isoquant we can discover which of firms 2 and 3 will be used to produce the extra 50 units of output. When the isocost line is steeper than the isoquant, firm 2 will be chosen. When the isocost line is less steep than the isoquant, then firm 3 will be used. When the isocost line has the same slope as the isoquant, then either (or both) firms could be used.

This somewhat strange isoquant is of course an extreme case. If there were a very large number of firms then the isoquant would begin to take on a more familiar shape. To see this we need to consider a more general case:

### A more general case

Let us now consider an industry with the following characteristics.

**TABLE 8.2**
**Input Coefficients and Capacity for Seven Firms in a Hypothetical Industry**

| Firm no. | $\xi_L$ | $\zeta_E$ | Capacity |
|---|---|---|---|
| 1 | 0.22 | 0.46 | 50 |
| 2 | 1.05 | 1.1 | 25 |
| 3 | 0.50 | 1.30 | 100 |
| 4 | 0.76 | 0.90 | 200 |
| 5 | 1.0 | 2.1 | 20 |
| 6 | 0.35 | 1.4 | 100 |
| 7 | 0.95 | 0.83 | 100 |

Assume furthermore that we choose the following four price combinations shown below: (The cases with $P_L = 0$ or $P_E = 0$ are chosen to obtain the borders of the substitution region. If we choose $P_L = 0$, this means that the only scarce factor is energy and hence firms are ordered on basis of their energy coefficient only. For every output level we then obtain the point with the lowest energy consumption possible. If we choose $P_E = 0$, we obtain the labour scarce border of the substitution region.)

| Case 1 | Case 2 | Case 3 | Case 4 |
|--------|--------|--------|--------|
| $P_L = 0$ | $P_L = 1$ | $P_L = 2$ | $P_L = 1$ |
| $P_E = 1$ | $P_E = 1$ | $P_E = 1$ | $P_E = 0$ |

From Table 8.2 we are now able to calculate the marginal (or average variable) cost for each firm in each of these cases. We could then *order* the firms according to their unit cost, an ordering which we know is the same as the order they appear in the industry production function as output expands. This order, based on the cases in Table 8.2, are shown in Table 8.3.

## TABLE 8.3
## Firms Ordered According to MC

| Case 1 | Case 2 | Case 3 | Case 4 |
|--------|--------|--------|--------|
| 1 | 1 | 1 | 1 |
| 7 | 4 | 6 | 6 |
| 4 | 6 | 3 | 3 |
| 2 | 7 | 4 | 4 |
| 3 | 3 | 7 | 7 |
| 6 | 5 | 2 | 5 |
| 5 | 2 | 5 | 2 |

Using Table 8.3 we can now calculate aggregate factor demands at different output levels for each of the four price ratios. For instance, for output level $Q = 400$ and for price ratio 1 we have full capacity production in firms 1, 7, 4, 2 (which makes a total of 375 units) and 25 per cent capacity utilisation in firm 3. In Figure 8.5, we have illustrated the isoquants for $Q = 100, 300$ and $500$ units, based on the data in Table 8.2.

**FIGURE 8.5**

**Isoquants for the Short-run Function Based on Table 8.2 (see text)**

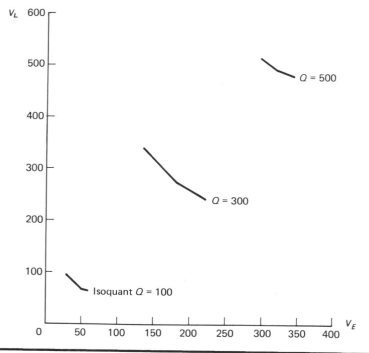

In this case, the isoquants consist of *two* line segments only, but this of course need not always be the case. Once again as the isocost line rotates the choice of inputs will switch from one end of the isoquant to the centre point of the isoquant and then to the other end of the isoquant.

## 8.8 The Elasticity of Scale

The construction of a short-run industry function is based on an *ordering* of individual firms according to their efficiencies. A firm's efficiency depends on (i) its input coefficients and (ii) the input prices. The simple rule of construction states that the most profitable firm (the one with lowest ratio variable cost/price) will always produce 'first', then the second most profitable comes in and so on up to full capacity.

This efficiency (or cost) ordering of firms implies that average variable cost increases with output and we can draw a parallel between this increase in average variable cost and output and our previously defined elasticity of 'scale'.

For our previous production functions we have:

$$\varepsilon_{qF} = 1/\varepsilon_{cq}$$

where $\varepsilon_{qF}$ is the elasticity of output $(q)$ with respect to equiproportionate changes in input $(F)$ (i.e. returns to scale)

$$\varepsilon_{qF} = \frac{dq}{q} \bigg/ \frac{dF}{F}$$

And $\varepsilon_{cq}$ is the elasticity of average cost with respect to changes in output with given prices

$$\varepsilon_{cq} = \frac{dc}{c} \bigg/ \frac{dq}{q}$$

Since we have ordered our firms in terms of increasing average variable cost it must be the case that expanding output leads to higher average variable cost and hence decreasing returns to scale. This is true for all expansion paths. Furthermore, since for the 'first' firm it is clear that $dc/dq$ (marginal cost) equals $c/q$ (average variable cost) hence

$$\varepsilon_{cq} = \frac{dc}{dq} \bigg/ \frac{c}{q} = \frac{c}{q} \bigg/ \frac{c}{q} = 1$$

It is to be observed, however, that the elasticity of scale discussed here is an *ex-post elasticity* where capital is excluded. It must also be observed that the elasticity of scale varies not only with output but also with the chosen factor price ratio.

It is not possible (in general) to obtain a simple equation for the elasticity of scale for a given short-run industry function. The function is not summarised in an algebraic formulae. The elasticities of scale and/or cost can be calculated only for certain points by calculating the ratio between marginal and average cost (for one specific input price ratio) for some output levels from zero up to full capacity.

The pairs of points $\varepsilon_{cq}$, $Q$ thus obtained could then be used for a statistical estimation of a continuous relation between $\varepsilon_{cq}$ and $Q$.

## 8.9   The Elasticity of Substitution

The technology of each firm is characterised by fixed input coefficients which makes substitution between factors of production impossible at the micro level. But substitution is still possible at the industry level since it is possible to choose different combinations of firms when producing a given amount of industry output. Industry substitution is therefore substitution *between* plants with different fixed, short-run technologies.

It is, however, not easy to obtain simple measures for the degree of substitutability in a short-run function. Each isoquant consists of a number of straight line segments and our derivative-based definition of the elasticity of substitution:

$$\sigma = \mathrm{d}(\ln FP)/\mathrm{d}(\ln \mathrm{SLOPE})$$

is obviously not directly applicable.

One way forward is to obtain approximations of the elasticity of substitution with the help of statistical estimation. For each isoquant we can calculate the SLOPE of each line segment. We can also calculate the factor proportions ($FP$) as the ratio between factors at the middle of the segment. These pairs of points can be used to calculate elasticities of each segment and we can then regress slope of FP to obtain a 'statistically' estimated elasticity of substitution.

$$\ln FP = a_0 + a_1 \cdot \ln \mathrm{SLOPE} \tag{8.13}$$

where $a_0$ and $a_1$ are estimated through ordinary linear regression. The estimate of $a_1$ is then obviously an estimate of the elasticity of substitution

These last two notions, scale elasticity and elasticity of substitution are not obvious summary statistics for production possibilities of the Johansen type. Nevertheless the Johansen model would give rise to certain observations of output, inputs and costs and these observations may be applied to estimating neoclassical production functions. They will in other words generate 'statistical' equivalents of these elasticities. These last two sections merely show how such results are to be interpreted in the Johansen framework.

## Appendix: The Houthakker Model

The form of the 'industry' or aggregate production function will obviously depend on the distribution of input coefficients in the $(\xi_L, \xi_E)$ space.

Imagine for a moment an economy in which the $\xi_L$, $\xi_E$ space is dense with machines so that there is a machine in existence for every $\xi_L, \xi_E$ combination. The output of any such machine is a function of its position in the $\xi_L$, $\xi_E$ space and Houthakker (1955–6) imposes further assumption that the distribution of 'capacity' outputs over $\xi_L$, $\xi_E$ is describable by a Pareto distribution such that

$$q = A \, \xi_L^{\alpha_1 - 1} \xi_E^{\alpha_2 - 2} \qquad (A8.1)$$

where $\alpha_1 > 1$, $\alpha_2 > 2$.

This implies that

(i) If either variable is absent then capacity is zero, that is there are no machines capable of producing without both inputs.
(ii) The further from the origin the larger is the capacity, that is machines with high $\xi_L$ and $\xi_E$ produce more.

This distribution of machines is assumed to be given and fixed and in order to derive a 'mean' production function from this set of fixed coefficient 'micro' units it is necessary to know which machines are in use and which are idle. The inputs and outputs of the machines in use can then be aggregated to yield the aggregate, 'mean', function.

Machines will be in use if they are capable of earning profits and will be idle otherwise. The dividing line is the zero quasi-rent line and depends on prices. Thus:

$$\text{Profit} = \pi = qP - P_L L - P_E E \qquad (A8.2)$$

Therefore for zero profits and letting $P$ be the numeraire we have:

$$1 = P_L \frac{L}{q} + P_E \frac{E}{q} \qquad (A8.3)$$

But $L/q = \xi_L$ and $E/q = \xi_E$, therefore

$$1 = P_L \xi_L + P_E \xi_E$$

Therefore

$$\xi_L = \frac{1}{P_L} - \frac{P_E}{P_L} \xi_E \qquad \text{(A8.4)}$$

Equation (A8.4) yields all those combinations of $\xi_L$ and $\xi_E$ which yield zero quasi rents. Hence those combinations represent the dividing line between active and idle machines. Diagrammatically we have (Figure 8.6):

**FIGURE 8.6**

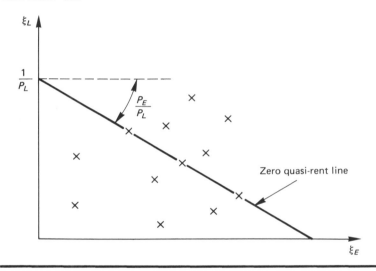

All machines which have input–output coefficients ($\xi_L$ and $\xi_E$) on or below the zero quasi-rent line will be operating a full capacity whereas all machines with coefficients above the zero quasi-rent line will be idle.

The set of machines in operation can therefore be perfectly determined by (a) the distribution of capacities over ($\xi_L, \xi_E$) and (b) the relative prices ($P_L$ and $P_E$).

Integrating over all machines which lie below the zero quasi-rent line yields aggregate output, aggregate labour input and aggregate energy input. These three aggregates are related by:

$$Q = \lambda \cdot L^{\alpha_1/(\alpha_1 + \alpha_2 + 1)} E^{\alpha_2/(\alpha_1 + \alpha_2 + 1)} \tag{A8.5}$$

where $\lambda$ is a constant.

This is very similar to the Cobb–Douglas function with decreasing returns to scale. The burden of this is that a fixed (micro) coefficient world can give rise to an aggregate Cobb–Douglas function if the micro units are distributed in a particular way (Pareto distribution) and if the zero quasi-rent line moves about depending on prices.

## Selected Reading

The standard reference for this chapter is of course L. Johansen, *Production Functions* (1972). Empirical applications of Johansen's production model can be found in F. Førsund, L. Hjalmarsson, S. Gaunitz and S. Wibe, 'Technical Progress and Structural Change in the Swedish Pulp Industry 1920–74' (1980), in T. Puu and S. Wibe (eds), *The Economics of Technological Progress*, and in W. Hildebrand, 'Short-run Production Functions based on Micro Data' (1981) *Econometrica*, Vol. 49. The Houthakker model was presented in the article by H. Houthakker, 'The Pareto Distribution and the Cobb–Douglas Production Function in Activity Analysis' (1955–6), *Review of Economics and Statistics*.

# Empirical Work on Production Functions

# 9

## 9.1 Introduction

Having a wide range of functional forms to choose among is obviously helpful when conducting *qualitative* investigations into questions of economic growth, income distribution, international trade and so on. However, it is often the case that some *quantitative* predictions are necessary. It is, for example, necessary to know the elasticity of substitution of the CES function before it will yield any information about the effect of wage increases on employment. This raises the question of how best to quantify the parameter values of the chosen functional form.

There are two possible ways forward here. First there is the 'statistical' or 'econometric' approach and second there is the 'direct' or 'engineering' approach.

The statistical approach is based on the idea that a process can adequately be described by examining its outputs and its inputs. It is not necessary to know anything about the 'science' involved in the process, all that is needed is a set of reliable observations of what goes in and what comes out. The parameter values are then inferred from these observations.

The engineering approach, however, requires no observations of inputs and outputs but does require a knowledge of the science being applied in the process. In order to know the production possibilities of a particular process it is necessary, therefore, to enquire of the applied scientist or engineer. He should know since he designed or is about to design the process itself.

These two approaches to quantification, econometric and engineering will be considered in turn.

## 9.2 The Econometric Approach

As we have said, this approach relies on our extracting information about the production function from actual observations of inputs and outputs. In an ideal world we would be able to do this with very few observations indeed. In the case of the Cobb–Douglas function, for example, we have that:

$$\text{Log } q = \text{Log } A + \alpha \text{ Log } V_1 + \beta \text{ Log } V_2 \tag{9.1}$$

Thus there are three 'unknowns'; $A$, $\alpha$ and $\beta$. With three independent observations of $(q, V_1$ and $V_2)$ we could therefore find these unknowns. Say, for example, we observe the following 'triples':

### TABLE 9.1

| Log $q$ | Log $V_1$ | Log $V_2$ |
|---------|-----------|-----------|
| 4       | 3         | 3         |
| 5.7     | 4         | 5         |
| 6.4     | 5         | 7         |

Substituting these into (9.1) yields:

$$\begin{aligned}
4 &= \text{Log } A + 3\alpha + 3\beta \\
5.7 &= \text{Log } A + 4\alpha + 5\beta \\
6.4 &= \text{Log } A + 5\alpha + 7\beta
\end{aligned} \tag{9.2}$$

(9.2) being three equations in three unknowns is solvable and yields, Log $A = 1$, $\alpha = 0.3$ and $\beta = 0.7$.

In order for this to work, it is necessary that the three equations (9.2) are 'independent', that is one of the equations is not a linear combination of the others. This raises a problem.

Typically the data come from examining the inputs and outputs of actual working processes (or firms). We could, at one moment in time, look at several processes each having the same production function. If there were '$n$' such firms then we would obtain '$n$' observations of ($q$, $V_1$ and $V_2$).

Alternatively, we could assume that a particular process (or firm) has the same production function over time. By periodically sampling inputs and outputs we could obtain a number of observations of ($q$, $V_1$ and $V_2$) as time went by. These observations could then be used to find the processes (or firms) production function.

The first (several firms approach) is called *cross-section* analysis. The second (single firm approach) is called *time series* analysis.

If we were to assume that '$n$' firms have a common production function which remained unchanged over time then we could combine the cross-section and time series data to yield 'panel' data.

This brings us to the difficulty mentioned earlier. If all the firms are identical and face the same set of prices then they will all choose the same ($q$, $V_1$ and $V_2$). Thus '$n$' firms would not yield '$n$' independent equations (9.2) but only one equation. In order to get independent observations firms must be assumed to face different prices.

The same problem does not extend to time series analysis. It is almost certain that the relative prices of capital and labour will change over time and the greater that change the greater will be the range of our observations of ($V_1$ and $V_2$).

## 9.3 Stochastic Equations

All the foregoing was posited on the assumption that we lived in a perfect world: an assumption which it is clearly necessary to relax.

One, possible source of imperfection is that our measurement of output might contain errors. Thus although $V_1$ and $V_2$ are known, our observations of $q$ comprise two parts; the true output of $q^*$ and the measurement error, say '$u$'. Therefore we have:

$$q^* = \text{Log } A + \alpha \text{ Log } V_1 + \beta \text{ Log } V_2 \qquad (9.1)$$

but $q^* = q - u$ and only $q$ is observed

$$q = \text{Log } A + \alpha \text{ Log } V_1 + \beta \text{ Log } V_2 + u \qquad (9.3)$$

The first three terms in the RHS of (9.3) constitute the 'deterministic' part $(q = A V_1{}^\alpha V_2{}^3)$. The final term $(u)$ is the 'stochastic' term or 'error' term. The deterministic part is derived from our economic theory and the error part from the inadequacy of our measurement. The problems of obtaining values for $A$, $\alpha$ and $\beta$ are now made much more difficult and a whole new area of expertise becomes necessary. This is the field of *econometrics* and it is no part of our present purpose to deal with econometrics. It is, however, necessary to know something of the way in which economic theory affects the econometric problem and the way in which econometric techniques alter the significance of what is done by the economic theorist. This should also provide some understanding of the reasons why the same data set can give rise to different estimates of the parameters.

## 9.4  The Error Structure

We have seen in the previous chapters that there are many ways of specifying a production function and some of them are so general as to be capable of representing almost any data set. The real problem is that we know nothing of the error term $(u)$.

One of the most common assumptions about '$u$' is that it has a zero mean. Thus if there are '$n$' observations of $(q, V_1, V_2)$ then:

$$E(u_i) = 0$$

Thus, errors sometimes result in overestimates of output and sometimes underestimate it, but over the years it is about right.

This assumption may seem innocuous enough but there is an immediate problem with it. This may be illustrated by reference to the Cobb–Douglas function:

$$q = A V_1^\alpha V_2^\beta$$

which can clearly be equivalently written as:

$$\log q = \text{Log } A + \alpha \text{ Log } V_1 + \beta \text{ Log } V_2$$

But this equivalence does not carry across to the stochastic case.

$$q = A V_1^\alpha V_2^\beta + u_1 \tag{9.4}$$

is not equivalent to

$$\log q = \text{Log } A + \alpha \text{ Log } V_1 + \beta \text{ Log } V_2 + u_2 \qquad (9.5)$$

if $u_1$ and $u_2$ are both assumed to have a mean of zero.

Thus, the introduction of the error term and the assumption that it has a zero mean restricts the range of legitimate manipulations which were possible for the deterministic equation.

## Some estimates

Quite a lot of early empirical work on the Cobb–Douglas function used the form (9.5). Douglas (1934) also constrained the estimates to have constant returns to scale. ($\alpha + \beta = 1$). Thus:

$$(\log q - \log V_2) = \log A + \alpha(\text{Log } V_1 - \text{Log } V_2) + u \ldots \qquad (9.6)$$

where $V_1$ is labour and $V_2$ is capital.

Equation (9.6) constrains $\alpha + \beta = 1$ and when applied to US manufacturing data for the period 1899–1922 (i.e. time series data) it yielded:

$$q = 1.01 \, V_1^{0.75} \, V_2^{0.25} \qquad (9.7)$$

$$\bar{R}^2 = 0.97$$

The $\bar{R}^2$ offers some indication of the explanatory power of the equation. If $V_1$ and $V_2$ together could exactly predict $q$ then $\bar{R}^2 = 1$. If they had absolutely no influence on $q$ then $\bar{R}^2 \to 0$. The $\bar{R}^2$ of 0.97 therefore suggest that 97 per cent of the variation in $q$ could be explained by variations in $V_1$ and $V_2$ and this leaves only 3 per cent as an 'error'.

These early estimates suggest that (or reflect the fact that) the share of output going to labour is 75 per cent and that going to capital is 25 per cent. It further suggests that the Cobb–Douglas function may be a 'good' representation of the process generating the observations.

Durand (1937) re-estimated (9.7) but relaxed the constant returns to scale assumption so that:

$$\log q = \text{Log } A + \alpha_1 \text{ Log } V_1 + \beta \text{ Log } V_2 + u$$

He found that:

$$q = 1.01 \, V_1^{0.765} \, V_2^{0.246}$$

From which it is clear that there are in fact constant returns to scale and that Douglas did no real violence by imposing it.

The effect of assuming a multiplicative exponential error term ($e^u$ was tested much later by Bodkin and Klein (1967) who used data for the US economy (excluding Government Services and Farming) for the period 1909–1949. They also included a technical progress term (see Chapter 7) thus

$$q = A e^{\lambda t} V_1^\alpha V_2^\beta e^u \tag{9.8}$$

and

$$q = A e^{\lambda t} V_1^\alpha V_2^\beta + u \tag{9.9}$$

They found

**TABLE 9.2**

|       | $\lambda$ | $\alpha$ | $\beta$ | $\bar{R}^2$ |
|-------|-----------|----------|---------|-------------|
| (9.8) | 0.00696   | 1.167    | 0.035   | 0.9925      |
| (9.9) | 0.00690   | 1.145    | 0.062   | 0.9899      |

This suggests that there are increasing returns to scale in both cases (9.8 and 9.9) but in neither case was the estimate of $\beta$ well determined. It further suggests that the parameter values are sensitive to the specification of the error term. Those found from (9.8) are not the same as those found from (9.9).

This result was supported by even later work by Mizon (1977). He used cross-sectional data for the UK (24 manufacturing industries) for 1960 to yield.

**TABLE 9.3**

|       | $\alpha$ | $\beta$ | $\bar{R}^2$ | $(\alpha + \beta)$ |
|-------|----------|---------|-------------|--------------------|
| $e^u$ | 0.7663   | 0.2438  | 0.939       | 1.010              |
| $+ u$ | 0.8312   | 0.1971  | 0.967       | 1.028              |

Both $\alpha$ and $\beta$ are well defined and, apart from yielding approximately constant returns to scale, reinforce the Bodkin and Klein result that changes in error specification will influence the estimated values of the parameters.

Of course, if we know that the only source of error is the measurement of $q$ then we can say something helpful about the error. That is, it is likely to be additive rather than multiplicative and exponential. Unfortunately there are many other sources of error. For example:

(i) *Inappropriate functional form.* In the experiments referred to above we imposed the Cobb–Douglas function on the data. The actual production function may or may not be of that form and any deviation from it will result in differences between the deterministic part of the equation $(A V_1^\alpha V_2^\beta)$ and the actual level of output ($q$). Thus even without measurement error there could still be an error term. In this case its form is much less clear.

(ii) *Omitted variables.* We have assumed that only $V_1$ and $V_2$ influence $q$ but it may be that some other variable also bears on output. An obvious candidate would be the effect of weather on farm production. Since we have omitted weather from the production function then and variation in it would cause $q$ to depart from $A V_1^\alpha V_2^\beta$. In this case the error may well be exponential and/or multiplicative.

(iii) *Error in Variables.* Measurement errors may well appear in the observations of $V_1$ and $V_2$ as well as in $q$, and implies a different treatment of the stochastic terms if those errors are correlated with $V_1$ and/or $V_2$. One solution to this problem would be to use '*instrumental variables*' (see Wonnacott and Wonnacott, 1970).

## 9.5  Simultaneous Equation Systems

It will be clear from earlier chapters that the production function is not an isolated equation but that it is embedded in a *system* of equations derived from hypotheses about the behaviour of entrepreneurs and the structure of markets. This can be illustrated by the Cobb–Douglas function, a profit-maximising entrepreneur and perfectly competitive markets. Thus:

$$q = A V_1^\alpha V_2^\beta \tag{9.10}$$

$$V_1 = \frac{\alpha P q}{P_1} \tag{9.11}$$

$$V_2 = \frac{\beta P q}{P_2} \tag{9.12}$$

where (9.10) is the production function and (9.11) and (9.12) are the derived 'first order' conditions or 'factor demand' equations.

From (9.11) and (9.12) we have:

$$\frac{V_1}{V_2} = \frac{\alpha P_2}{\beta P_1} \tag{9.13}$$

from which it is clear that when the relative prices of the factors are the same for all firms (cross-section) or are the same over time (time series) then the *ratio* of $V_1$ to $V_2$ will remain constant. That means that we get observations of $V_1$ and $V_2$ along only one ray of the production function. The data cannot therefore reveal anything about the substitution possibilities between $V_1$ and $V_2$ (cf. Section 9.2 above).

Two further consequences flow from these three equations (9.10), (9.11), (9.12). The first is that entrepreneurs decide $V_1$ and $V_2$ by reference to their prices. They take these prices as 'given' and choose $V_1$ and $V_2$ accordingly. Thus $V_1$ and $V_2$ are not 'exogenous' (given to the entrepreneur) they are 'endogenous' (determined within the system of equations). The exogenous variables are now $P$, $P_1$ and $P_2$.

Each of the three equations can have error terms associated with them and errors in '$q$' will influence the choice of $V_1$ and $V_2$. The errors of the three equations will not therefore be independent and the estimation procedure should recognise this. (see Zellner *et al.*, 1966).

The second consequence to flow from the system of equations (9.10), (9.11), (9.12), is that $\alpha$ and $\beta$ could be found from (9.10) or from the factor demand equations. (9.11) and (9.12). If, for example, we have observations of $V_1$, $P$, $q$ and $P_1$ then via (9.11) we can easily find $\alpha$. Similarly for $\beta$ and (9.12). Thus we have two ways of determining $\alpha$ and $\beta$ and it is necessary to use all equations if the best estimates of $\alpha$ and $\beta$ are to be found. Thus the three equations have to be estimated *simultaneously* so that $\alpha$ and $\beta$ are chosen to satisfy them. These simultaneous estimates have also to bear in mind the alternative error specifications for each equation (multiplicative or additive), and the possible interdependence of the errors.

The Bodkin and Klein article referred to earlier also contains results of estimating $\alpha$ and $\beta$ by simultaneous equations in which the prices are regarded as exogenous. Their *two* equations are:

$$q = A^{\lambda t} V_1^{\alpha} V_2^{\beta}$$

$$\frac{V_1}{V_2} = \frac{\alpha P_2}{\beta P_1}$$

each with either additive or multiplicative errors.

**TABLE 9.4**

|  | $\alpha$ | $\beta$ | $\lambda$ | $\bar{R}^2$ |
|---|---|---|---|---|
| $\cdot e^u$ | 0.960 | 0.496 | 0.00484 | 0.9795 |
| $+ u$ | 0.964 | 0.501 | 0.00526 | 0.9811 |

These estimates of $\alpha$ and $\beta$ yield the results shown in Table 9.4 and show reasonable comparability between the two specifications with both having high $\bar{R}^2$, technical progress of about 0.5 per cent per annum and returns to scale of $\simeq 1.46$. These results do, however, differ substantially from the Bodkin and Klein single equation estimates of $\alpha$ and $\beta$ in Table 9.2.

### Estimating the CES function

The first order conditions have been used in a rather different way in the case of the CES function. In one form it may be written:

$$q^{-\theta} = \gamma[\delta V_1^{-\theta} + (1 - \delta)V_2^{-\theta}] \qquad (9.14)$$

This, with either error term, cannot be linearised simply by taking logs. If linear regression analysis is to be used then the econometrician has to find some way of linearising (9.14).

The approach used by its originators (Arrow, Chenery, Minhas and Solow (ACMS)) was to do a *stepwise* regression, beginning with the first order condition for labour $V_1$ and using the results from that to linearise (9.14). The first order condition for labour from (9.14) is

$$\log\left(\frac{q}{V_1}\right) = \cdot \sigma \log \gamma\delta + \sigma \log\left(\frac{P_1}{P}\right) \tag{9.15}$$

where $\sigma = 1/1 - \theta$ = elasticity of substitution.

This is linear, at least as it is written (in logs), and hence a linear regression will yield estimates of $\sigma \log \gamma\delta$ and of $\sigma$. This estimate of $\sigma$ then enables $\theta$ to be calculated and values for $q^{-\theta}$, $V_1^{-\theta}$ and $V_2^{-\theta}$ to be constructed.

These values can be inserted into (9.14) to yield a linear equation in $(q^{-\theta}, V_1^{-\theta}$ and $V_2^{-\theta})$ which yields estimates of $\gamma$ and $\delta$.

Of course if $\sigma$ turns out to be 1 from (9.15) then there is no need to further investigate the CES since $\sigma = 1$ implies a Cobb–Douglas function. But ACMS found that $\sigma$ differed from 1 (see Arrow *et al.*, 1961).

This stepwise procedure is not optimal since $\sigma$ is not chosen to give the best fit with (9.14) *and* (9.15). Indeed if the $V_2$ factor demand equation had been used to estimate $\sigma$ then a quite different value for $\sigma$ may have resulted.

An alternative way of linearising the CES function is due to Kmenta (1967).

He linearised the CES function by taking a Maclaurin's series expansion of it around $\theta = 0$.

Thus: since there are constant returns to scale the CES function may be written as:

$$\left(\frac{q}{v_2}\right) = \gamma\left[\delta\left(\frac{v_1}{v_2}\right)^{-\theta} + (1-\delta)\right]^{(1/\theta)} \tag{9.16}$$

Therefore

$$\log\left(\frac{q}{v_2}\right) = \log\gamma - \frac{1}{\theta}\log\left[\delta\left(\frac{v_1}{v_2}\right)^{-\theta} + (1-\delta)\right] \tag{9.17}$$

let

$$\log\left[\delta\left(\frac{v_1}{v_2}\right)^{-\theta} + (1-\delta)\right] = f(\theta)$$

by Maclaurin's theorem

$$f(\theta) = f(0) + \frac{f_1(0)\theta}{1} + \frac{f_2(0)\theta^2}{2} + R \tag{9.18}$$

where $f(0)$ is the function $f(\theta)$ evaluated at $\theta = 0$, $f_1(0)$ is the first derivative of the function $f(\theta)$ wrt $(\theta)$ again evaluated at $\theta = 0, f_2(0)$ is the second derivative of the function $f(\theta)$ wrt $(\theta)$ evaluated at $\theta = 0$ and $R$ is the remainder (considered negligible).

$$f(0) = \log\left[\delta\left(\frac{v_1}{v_2}\right)^{-0} + (1-\delta)\right]$$

$$= \log(\delta + 1 - \delta)$$

$$= \log 1 = 0$$

$$f_1(\theta) = -\left[\delta\left(\frac{v_1}{v_2}\right)^{-\theta} + (1-\delta)\right]^{-1}\delta\left(\frac{v_1}{v_2}\right)^{-\theta}\log\left(\frac{v_1}{v_2}\right)$$

therefore

$$f_1(0) = -\delta.\log\left[\frac{v_1}{v_2}\right]$$

and

$$f_2(\theta) = -\left[\delta\left(\frac{v_1}{v_2}\right)^{-\theta} + (1-\delta)\right]^{-2}\left[\delta\left(\frac{v_1}{v_2}\right)^{-\theta}\log\left(\frac{v_1}{v_2}\right)^2\right]$$

$$+ \left[\delta\left(\frac{v_1}{v_2}\right)^{-\theta} + (1-\delta)\right]^{-1}\delta\left(\frac{v_1}{v_2}\right)^{-\theta}\left(\log\frac{v_1}{v_2}\right)^2$$

therefore

$$f_2(0) = \log\left(\frac{v_1}{v_2}\right)^2(-\delta^2 + \delta) = \log\left(\frac{v_1}{v_2}\right)^2\delta(\delta-1)$$

Putting all these terms into (9.18) and ignoring $R$ yields:

$$\log\left(\frac{q}{v_2}\right) = \log\gamma + \delta\log\left(\frac{v_1}{v_2}\right) + \theta\delta(1-\delta)\left[\log\left(\frac{v_1}{v_2}\right)\right]^2 \qquad (9.19)$$

This is the Kmenta approximation to the CES with constant returns to scale. As can be seen when $\theta = 0$, (9.19) reduces to the Cobb–Douglas case. (It also is the CRTS case of the translog function.)

The equivalent for returns to scale $\mu$ becomes:

$$\text{Log } q = \text{Log}\gamma + \delta\mu\,\text{Log } V_1 + \left(\frac{1}{\mu} - \delta\mu\right)\text{Log } V_2$$

$$+ \delta(1-\delta)\mu\theta\left[\text{Log }\frac{V_1}{V_2}\right]^2$$

So when $\mu = 1$

$$\text{Log } q = \text{Log } \gamma + \delta \text{ Log } V_1 + \text{Log } V_2 - \delta \text{ Log } V_2$$
$$+ \delta(1-\delta)\theta\left[\text{Log }\frac{V_1}{V_2}\right]^2$$

that is

$$\text{Log }\frac{q}{V_2} = \text{Log } \gamma + \delta \text{ Log }\frac{V_1}{V_2} + \theta\delta(1-\delta)\left[\text{Log }\frac{V_1}{V_2}\right]^2 \qquad (9.20)$$

*Note*: Equation (9.19) is an approximation to the CES *around the point* $\theta = 0$. As $\theta$ departs from 0 the remainder term becomes more important and hence (9.19) can only really be used to test whether $\theta$ is 0 or not or at any rate is confined to values of $\theta$ very close to the Cobb–Douglas case.

The stepwise procedure of ACMS and the linearisation proposed by Kmenta therefore both have their disadvantages. ACMS by not making the best use of the economic theory and Kmenta by having only a limited range of $\sigma$ over which it is valid.

It is of course no longer necessary to go to such lengths to achieve a linear model (or equation). Mizon (1977) uses non-linear estimation methods to estimate

$$q = \gamma[\delta V_1^{-\theta} + (1-\delta)V_2^{-\theta}]^{-\mu/\theta} + e$$

for the 1960 UK manufacturing cross-section data referred to above. His estimates are:

$$\sigma = 1.381, \qquad \mu = 1.0372, \qquad \delta = 0.1918, \qquad \gamma = 1.0527$$
$$R^2 = 0.9652$$

Thus the elasticity of substitution ($\sigma$) is greater than unity, there are constant returns to scale ($\mu$) and very little output going to capital ($\delta$). For the US Bodkin and Klein (1967) estimated CES functions in the same way as they did for Cobb-Douglas functions (see above). They tried single equation estimates with additive and multiplicative errors and they tried two-equation models with additive and multiplicative errors. Their results are shown in Table 9.5.

There are many possible explanations of the difference between the greater than unity estimates of $\sigma$ reported for the UK reported by Mizon and the much less than unity estimates reported by Bodkin and Klein.

Bodkin and Klein used time series data whereas Mizon used cross-section data but the original work on the CES by ACMS used cross-

## TABLE 9.5

|  | $\sigma$ | $\delta$ | $\mu$ | $\lambda$ | $\bar{R}^2$ |
|---|---|---|---|---|---|
| Single with $\times e^u$ | 0.0944 | 0.9975 | 1.210 | 0.00675 | 0.9926 |
| Single with $+ u_u$ | 0.0894 | 0.9992 | 1.220 | 0.00663 | 0.9900 |
| Simultaneous with $\times e^u$ | 0.4694 | 0.6037 | 1.238 | 0.00643 | 0.9804 |
| Simultaneous with $+ u$ | 0.6780 | 0.4471 | 1.362 | 0.00589 | 0.9834 |

Where $\sigma$ is the elasticity of substitution, $\delta$ is the distribution parameter on capital, $\mu$ are returns to scale, $\lambda$ is the rate of technical progress.

sectional US data and found elasticities of substitution almost everywhere less than unity (ACMS, 1961).

These remarks apply to the single equation estimates but there are also wide differences within the Bodkin and Klein results. Once again it is apparent that the same data set and same production function yield quite different estimates of its parameters simply by recognising the importance of the correct specification of the error structure.

It should be remembered that the first order conditions were introduced into the 'system' on the assumption of profit maximising entrepreneurs operating in perfectly competitive markets. These assumptions, particularly the latter are very strong indeed and hence some of the differences reported by Bodkin and Klein may arise from there being imperfect competition in factor and/or product markets.

There is a further problem if the perfectly competitive market assumption is dropped. If there is an imperfect market for $v_1$ for example, then there will be an upward sloping supply curve for $v_1$ ss shown in Figure 9.1. This gives another equation relating $P_1$ to $v_1$ say

$$P_1 \equiv v_1^{p_1 - 1} \tag{9.21}$$

Thus from (9.21) we have a positive relation between $P_1$ and $v_1$ but from (9.15) (the factor demand equation) we have a negative relation between $P_1$ and $v_1$. This raises the *identification problem*. If $v_1$ is regressed on $P_1$ is the result an estimate of the demand curve (9.15) or of the supply curve (9.21)?

**FIGURE 9.1**

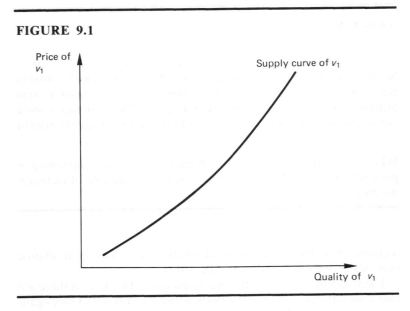

If changes in $P_1$ are caused by movements of the supply curve, then they will provide estimates of the demand curve. If, however, the changes are due to movements of the demand curve (say due to changes in $q$), then they will provide estimates of the supply curve. This may be made clearer by the diagrammatic example shown in Figure 9.2

In Figure 9.2(a) the supply curve takes four positions yielding observations $(P_1, v_{11})$, $(P_2, v_{12})$, $(P_3, v_{13})$, $(P_4, v_{14})$ which all lie on the demand curve and hence are suitable for estimating (9.15).

On the other hand, Figure 9.2(b) shows the fixed supply curve and four different positions of the demand curve. The four observations of $P$ and $v_1$ are now all lying on the supply curve and cannot be used to augment our information about 'α' via equation (9.15).

When *both* the supply and the demand curves are moving then the observations lie on neither the demand curve nor the supply curve and can be used only if the movements can be *identified*. Econometric texts provide the rules for ensuring that this identification requirement can be satisfied by the system of equations under consideration.

**FIGURE 9.2(a)**

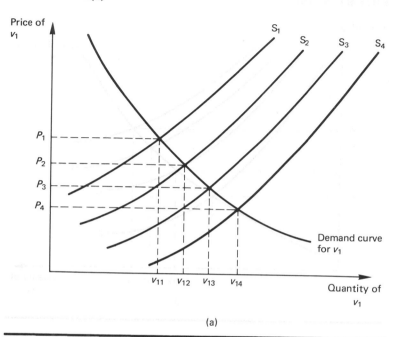

(a)

## 9.6 Estimating the Translog Production Function

Recall that the translog production function takes the form:

$$\log q = \log \gamma_0 + \alpha_1 \log v_1 + \beta_1 \log v_2 + \alpha_2 (\log v_1)^2 \qquad (9.22)$$
$$+ \beta_2 (\log v_2)^2 + \gamma_1 \log v_1 \log_2$$

which is linear in parameters and hence least squares estimates are easily obtained. There is, however, a simple alternative to estimating (9.22) directly.

We have that:

$$\frac{\partial \log q}{\partial \log v_1} = \frac{\partial q}{\partial v_1} \cdot \frac{v_1}{q}$$

**FIGURE 9.2(b)**

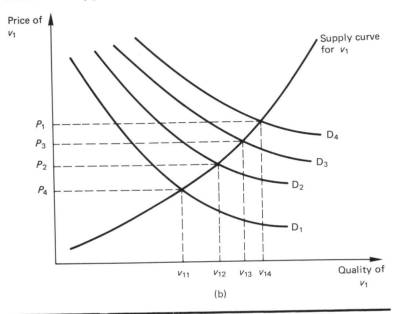

(b)

For profit max in perfectly competitive markets we also have that:

$$\frac{\partial q}{\partial v_1} = \frac{P_1}{P}$$

Therefore

$$\frac{\partial \log q}{\partial \log v_1} = \frac{\partial q}{\partial v_1} \frac{v_1}{q}$$

$$= \frac{P_1 \cdot v_1}{P \cdot q}$$

$$= \text{share of } v_1 \text{ in the total revenues}$$

From (9.22)

$$\frac{\partial \log q}{\partial \log v_1} = \alpha_1 + 2\alpha_2 \log v_1 + \gamma_1 \log v_2 \tag{9.23}$$

Thus in our (9.23) we can obtain estimates of $\alpha_1, \alpha_2$ and $\gamma_1$. Repeating this for $v_2$ yields $\beta_1, \beta_2$ and $\gamma_1$. A similar argument can be advanced if the translog cost function rather than the production function is being used. Recall that the translog cost function is (see (9.14)):

$$\log C = \log \delta_0 + \gamma_1 \log q + \log P_2 + \alpha_1 \log \left(\frac{P_1}{P_2}\right)$$

$$+ \gamma_2 (\log q)^2 + \frac{\delta_3}{2} \left(\log \frac{P_1}{P_2}\right)^2 + \delta_1 \log q \log\left(\frac{P_1}{P_2}\right) \quad (9.24)$$

We also have by Shephard's lemma that

$$\frac{\partial C}{\partial P_i} = v_i \text{ where } v_i \text{ is the cost minimising level of input } v_i$$

Therefore

$$\frac{\partial \log C}{\partial \log P_1} = \frac{\partial C}{\partial P_1} \frac{P_1}{C} = \frac{v_1 P_1}{C}$$

$$= \text{share of input } v_1 \text{ in total cost } (C) \text{ of production}$$

Hence

$$\frac{v_1 P_1}{C} = \alpha_1 + \delta_3 \log P_1 - \delta_3 \log P_2 + \delta_1 \log q \quad (9.25)$$

Thus (9.25) yields estimates of $\alpha_1, \delta_3$ and $\delta_1$ (see for example Berndt and Christensen, 1973).

The exercise can be repeated for $v_2$.

*Note*: This translog cost function does not imply a translog production function. But if both the translog production function and the translog cost functions are regarded as approximations to the same underlying technology, then both may be used (see Burgess, 1975).

Notice too that the cost function chosen does not imply CRTS for the underlying production function.

The net result of this, somewhat brief survey of the econometric problems is that introducing the stochastic term into the production function is fraught with difficulty. The form of the error term, the allocation of the error among the variables in each equation, the choice of instrumental variables, the use of the first order conditions to augment the information on the parameters, the simultaneous equation estimates and the identification problem all require the exercise of judgement as well as an understanding of econometrics. In the face of such difficulties it may seem easier to adopt the alternative – the engineering approach.

## 9.7 The Engineering Approach

The only effective alternative to the statistical approach to empirical production functions is the engineering approach. This method was advanced in the late 1940s by H. B. Chenery who was convinced that a more engineering-oriented approach would improve the quality of empirical production studies. Briefly stated, the engineering approach implies that observable input–output points do not constitute a (or the only) source of information on production technology. Instead, theoretical production data are constructed from engineering descriptions of processes. Thus, instead of reading production statistics, the investigator has to consult engineers, read blueprints, engineering theory and so forth. From this direct information, the economist has to construct the ordinary production function.

## 9.8 The Formal Structure of Engineering Analysis

Perhaps the greatest difficulty with engineering analyses is the use of non-economic variables. The economic production function relates flows of input to a flow of output and each quantity can be assigned a unique price. Things are much more complicated in the engineering world where we cannot find a common dimension for all variables. For instance, an engineering description might work with variables like speed, strength, stability, viscosity etc. For these, and similar, variables it is rather meaningless to talk about 'quantities', in the ordinary sense of the word. Accordingly, it is also meaningless to try to derive 'shadow-prices' for all the engineering variables which enter an engineering description.

The relation between engineering descriptions and the economic production function can be illustrated with the help of a formal model. Let us assume that we need '$n$' different engineering variables to define a process. Assume further that all these variables can be numerically represented by $x_1, \ldots, x_n$. Usually it takes several hundreds of equations to give an accurate engineering description of a production process, but for the sake of simplification we shall here assume that all these can be comprised into one single equation:

$$q = e(x_1, \ldots, x_n) \tag{9.26}$$

where $q$, as usual, is the quantity of output. This relation, $q = (x)$, is called an *engineering production function.*

Now we assume that we have '$m$' different economic factors (such as energy, capital, etc.) the quantities of which we denote $v_1, \ldots, v_m$. A specific choice of engineering variables also determines the use of economic factors through the relations:

$$v_j = h_j(x_1, \ldots, x_n) \qquad j = 1, \ldots, m \tag{9.27}$$

We call these relations *input functions.*

Input functions of the type (9.27) are of course an immense simplification of the real world relations between engineering variables and economic factors. However, if we accept the formulation (9.27), we can formulate the technical optimality problem as:

$$\text{Max } q = e(x_1, \ldots, x_n) \tag{9.28}$$

S.T.

$$v_j = h_j(x_1, \ldots, x_n) \qquad j = 1, \ldots, m$$

For each set of economic factors $v_1, \ldots, v_m$, the solution of (9.28) yields the optimum rate of production, $q$. Accordingly, the total solution to (9.28) is the economic production fucntion $q = f(v_1, \ldots, v_m)$. By solving optimality problem for many sets of economic factors, we can obtain as many points on the economic production function as we like.

Equation (9.28) is formulated as a maximisation problem. However, it is often more convenient to formulate the problem as one of minimising – costs, given a specific level of output. Assuming that $q$ is the desired level of output (e.g. the desired capacity of a plant to be built) and that $P_1, \ldots, P_m$ are the prices of inputs, we can formulate the problem:

$$\text{Min } C = P_1 v_1 + , \ldots, + P_m v_m$$

S.T.

$$\bar{q} = e(x, \ldots, x_n) \tag{9.29}$$

$$v_j = h_j(x_1, \ldots, x_n)$$

The solution to this problem yields for each set of prices an input configuration $v_1, \ldots, v_m$, that is a point on the production isoquant $q = \bar{q}$.

## 9.9 An Illustrative Example of Engineering Functions

The engineering approach is usually alien to the economist way of thinking, and an illustrative example might help to understand the character of the problem. For this example we assume the simplest case possible. We assume that (i) the engineering production function is log-linear, (ii) the input functions are linear and (iii) the number of engineering variables equals the number of economic factors.

Let $\phi$ be the amount of a homogeneous output. Assume that output is a function of two engineering variables (the interpretation of which will be discussed later) $x_1$ and $x_2$, according to an ordinary Cobb–Douglas relation:

$$\phi = A x_1^{\alpha} x_2^{1-\alpha} \tag{9.30}$$

($A$ a constant $> 0$ and $0 < \alpha < 1$)

Assume further that one unit of $x_1$ requires $a_1$ of labour ($L$) and $a_3$ units of capital ($K$), and corresponding for $x_2$ such that:

$$L = a_1 x_1 + a_2 x_2$$
$$K = a_3 x_1 + a_4 x_2 \tag{9.31}$$

Let us for simplicity also assume that all $a_i > 0$.

By solving $x_1$ and $x_2$ and substituting into (9.30) we obtain a production function in the economic variables $K$ and $L$:

$$\phi = \frac{A}{(a_1 a_4 - a_2 a_3)} \cdot (a_1 K - a_3 L)^{1-\alpha} \cdot (a_4 L + a_2 K)^{\alpha} \tag{9.32}$$

Equation (9.30) is the engineering production function, and (9.31) the input functions. In principle, $x_1$ and $x_2$ could be interpreted as any engineering parameters, such as speed, length, height, etc. However, in this example $x_1$ and $x_2$ are interpreted as *numbers of different machines*. Total production can then be carried out by combining these machines according to the Cobb–Douglas formulation (9.30).

Furthermore, if $x_1$ are interpreted as machines, the interpretation of the input functions are obvious: (9.31) simply states that it takes $a_1$

units of labour and $a_3$ units of capital to operate machine 1 and the corresponding for machine 2.

It is not unrealistic to think of a process where two machines can be combined according to (9.30). When, for instance, cutting trees, one can choose between different machines (power-saws, large processors, etc.) suitable for different land conditions. Usually the natural environment is such that at least two kinds of machines must be used: large processors for large even areas and power-saws for selective cutting or for rough areas. In many other processes we find similar conditions, for example digging, grass-cutting, snow-clearance. etc.

The combination of (9.30) and (9.31) gives a very special combination of the 'neoclassical' and 'Leontief' assumptions regarding substitution possibilities between factors of production. Technically, the substitution possibilities are unlimited, while economically there exists bounded substitutability due to the fixed input coefficients. The substitution between labour and capital is made possible by substitution between different kinds of machines. In this respect the formulation should satisfy those economists arguing that a spade must be supported by one (and not three or one-third) man, as well as those who argue that a spade can always be substituted for an excavator.

It is worth noting that the economic production function (9.32) is not defined for the whole input space. If we assume that

$$a_1 a_4 - a_2 a_3 > 0$$

that is that machine 1 is more labour intensive than machine 2, we observe that (9.32) is only defined for the region where:

$$\frac{a_3}{a_1} \leqslant \frac{K}{L} \leqslant \frac{a_4}{a_2}$$

However, for some parts of this region the isoquants are positively sloped, and the economic substitution region (i.e. the region which is considered given non-negative prices and cost-minimising firms) is still more narrow. It can easily be shown that the substitution region is defined by

$$\frac{a_3 a_4}{a_1 a_4 \alpha + a_2 a_3 (1 - \alpha)} \leqslant \frac{K}{L} \leqslant \frac{a_1 a_4 (1 - \alpha) + a_2 a_3 \alpha}{a_1 a_2}$$

Two production isoquants are illustrated in Figure 9.3.

**FIGURE 9.3**
**Technical Isoquants Derived from the Production Function**

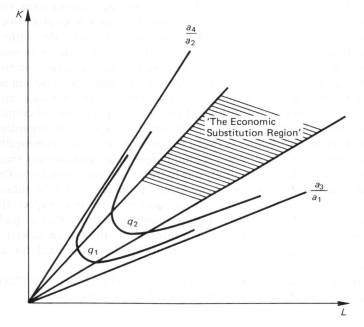

As we can see from the curvature of the isoquants, we have a function with a variable elasticity of substitution. If the elasticity $\sigma$, is calculated along an isoquant, we obtain:

$$\sigma = \frac{\left(a_3 a_4 - (a_1 a_4 \alpha + a_2 a_3 (1-\alpha)) \cdot \dfrac{K}{L}\right)\left(a_1 a_4 (1-\alpha) + a_1 a_3 - a_1 a_2 \cdot \dfrac{K}{L}\right)}{(a_1 a_4 - a_2 a_3)^2 \cdot \alpha(\alpha - 1) \cdot \dfrac{K}{L}}$$

and it is easy to see that $\sigma \geqslant 0$ inside the substitution region ($\sigma = 0$ on the boundary) and $\sigma < 0$, outside this region.

Our hypothetical example might also throw some light on the nature of *ex post* production functions. Instead of assuming that the amount of capital is fixed *ex post*, we could (more realistically) assume that capacity is fixed by the *number of machines* that is that

$$x_i \leqslant \bar{x}_i \qquad i = 1, 2 \tag{9.33}$$

This means that the firm has already bought $\bar{x}_i$ units of machine $i$, and cannot *ex post* exceed this number.

$K$ is now the amount of capital *used*, and can vary within the limits set by (9.33). If the cost of capital is independent of its use, then the *ex post* price is zero, and only the price of labour matters when analysing the economic optimum.

The new substitution region is illustrated in Figure 9.4.

---

**FIGURE 9.4**
**Illustration to the ex post Function when Restrictions are Placed on the Engineering Variables**

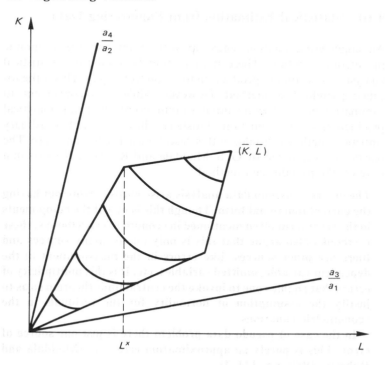

---

The *ex post* substitution region has the shape typical of Leif Johansen's *ex post* macro functions (see Chapter 8). There is also nothing preventing us from using the function as a macro function $\bar{x}_1$ and $\bar{x}_2$ would then denote total machine equipment in the industry. (It can even be more realistic to use the function as a macro function. For instance, if we think of tree cutting, some firms may only use mechine 1, while others use machine 2 (due, perhaps to natural conditions).)

If we assume that the *ex post* price of capital is zero, the firm will always choose the technology shown by the capital intensive boundary of the substitution region. The variable average cost $x$ will then be constant up to $L$ and thereafter increasing. Under certain reasonable assumptions we thus arrive at the ordinary 'neoclassical' cost curves. However, it is to be observed, that the U-shaped cost curves are caused by the bounded substitution regions, and not by a variable elasticity of scale.

## 9.10 Statistical Estimation from Engineering Data

An engineering analysis ends up with points on the economic production function. These points could be used for a statistical analysis with ordinary production function techniques. This is the so-called pseudo-data method. However, while it is convenient to summarise many discrete input–output points with an analytical production (or cost) function, statisticians have argued that ordinary statistical methods should, in this case, be used with great care. The reason was explained by G. S. Maddala and R. Blaine Roberts in a note on the pseudo-data method:

> The errors in pseudo data analysis arise entirely from not having the correct functional form. Though this is one of the components in the error term often mentioned in econometric textbooks, these textbooks also argue that this is only one of many sources and there are other sources, like errors in the measurement in the dependent variable, omitted variables, etc. It is this multiplicity of errors that enables one to invoke the central limit theorem so as to justify the assumption of normality for the residuals in the econometric equations.
>
> In the case of pseudo data problem there is just one source of error. This is purely an approximation error . . . (Maddala and Roberts, 1980, pp. 323–4).

According to Maddala and Roberts, the pseudo-data method would be very sensitive to the functional specification. They also provided an example which showed that many different production functions (Cobb–Douglas, CES, translog) could be fitted to the same data set with almost the same high correlation. However, predictions on price-elasticities, cost-shares etc. were quite different in the three cases, and Maddala and Roberts concluded that a good functional fit (measured for instance with a high $R^2$) was no guarantee for a correct representation of technology. Their conclusion was rather that it was best *not* to use ordinary statistical estimation techniques to summarise the results from an engineering model.

## 9.11  Merits and Drawbacks of the Engineering Approach

The solid foundation makes an engineering approach very appealing to a potential investigator. Production technology is directly calculated and no statistical errors can distort the results. It is also likely that the revealed part of the production function is bigger with the engineering approach, since observable data points include technologies considered optimal on basis of historical prices.

The engineering approach has, however, some serious drawbacks. The method is extremely time-consuming and a researcher has to devote perhaps years of study for the construction of an isoquant for some small process. This should be compared with the statistical method where complete cost and production functions for the whole economy can be calculated with a few weeks research.

There is also another, and perhaps more important, difference between the engineering and the statistical approach. Observable data are in one sense more reliable than hypothetical data. An observed input–output point represents something that has really happened, that is an actual behaviour which has taken place. This is not the case for pseudo-data. We might well construct an hypothetical isoquant on the basis of hypothetical prices, but we cannot know points on that isoquant really would be chosen if the hypothetical prices would 'come true'. An actual change in prices might lead to the marketing of a new machine which was not calculated in our engineering model and, as a result, new possible factor combinations would be revealed. Accordingly, the statistical approach represents *behaviour* in quite another sense than the engineering approach.

## 9.12 Empirical Engineering Production Functions

Empirical engineering production functions is something of a tautology, since engineering functions almost by definition are empirical. There is no uniform 'engineering theory' of production, at most there are some ideas of general structure of engineering analysis offered by the pioneer in the field, H. B. Chenery.

An engineering approach to production studies started before Chenery. Perhaps the first complete study with an engineering method was the study by Frisch (1935b) on the technology of chocolate production. In this study Frisch conducted a detailed mapping of the substitution between 'fat' and other costs.

In 1949 and in 1953 Chenery published his classic studies of engineering productions and functions involving, among other things, an empirical study of the technology of gas transmission. About ten years later, Hurther (1962) conducted an empirical analysis of a petroleum refinery using the engineering approach suggested by Chenery. Boon (1964) analysed capital-labour substitution in a number of discrete processes (ploughing, earth-moving, metal-turning, etc.) and the same substitution was studied by Lamyai (1978) in a penetrating analysis of a minor sub-process; the production of head lugs for bicycles. The production of oil tankers was studied by Eide (1979) and Wibe (1980) used the engineering approach to analyse the production of iron.

There is no sharp line between engineering studies and other empirical production analyses. The degree of engineering varies continuously from 0 to 1. Accordingly, to the list presented above, we could add some more or less partial engineering studies (such as Smith (1961), Kurtz and Manne (1963), Brown (1966), Belinfante (1969), De Salvo (1969), Cowing (1970), Marsden *et al.* (1974) and others). Also, in the agricultural area there has been a lot of 'engineering studies' on the technology of feeding chickens, growing crops, etc. (see for example Heady and Dillon, 1961).

One problem with engineering analysis has been the lack of economic content. Many writers seem to have forgotten that Chenery's method was advanced as a way to improve the quantitative aspect in production analyses. The aim was not to make engineers of economists. However, many engineering studies end with the establishment of the engineering relations and no attempt is made to summarise the information using economic concepts (such as elasticities of scale and substitution).

However, a number of modern studies have tried to use engineering plant models for generating production data which are then used for a statistical adaptation with economic production function. This is the so-called 'pseudo-data' method which was advanced by Griffin (1977b, 1978; 1979; 1980) and further analysed by Kopp and Smith (1980a, b; 1983; 1985) and by Wibe (1980). The pseudo-data method has the advantage of summarising engineering information into a statistical function where economic measures are easy to obtain. However, the statistical dangers with the pseudo-data method, as discussed in 9.11, should be borne in mind.

## 9.13 Empirical Best Practice Studies

The vast majority of best practice, or frontier, production studies are analyses of productive (in)-efficiency. The exception to this rule is a study by Førsund and Hjalmarsson (1979a) on technical progress in Swedish dairy plants. In this study the authors analyse progress both in the best practice and average practice production functions.

Empirical applications of the best practice concept started with a 1948 study by A. P. Grosse on open hearth steel furnaces. In this (and later on in Salter (1960) the term was reserved for a specific 'technique' rather than for a whole production function. The first to use a best practice function as an empirical concept was Farrell (1957) who wanted to measure empirically the productive efficiency of agriculture in different countries. Later on, best practice functions have been estimated by Aigner and Chu (1968) for US primary metal industry 1957–8. Aigner and Chu used the empirical material for illustration purposes only and the same data set was also used (with the same purpose) in the 1976 study by Aigner *et al*. In Richmond (1974) micro data from the Norwegian manufacturing industry (1963) was used in the estimation of frontier production functions of the Cobb–Douglas type, one for each industry. A Cobb–Douglas frontier function and plant data was also used by Meeusen and Broeck (1977) in their study of efficiency in the French industry. Basically the same approach was used by Lee and Tyler (1978) in the study of the efficiency of Brazilian industry. Lee and Tyler used data from 850 industrial firms in the estimation of one Cobb–Douglas production function. Finally, Timmer (1971) used annual data from the different states in the US 1960–67 in estimating a frontier production function for agriculture using labour, capital, land, fertilisers and livestock as factors of production.

Best practice technologies have also been studied empirically with the dual to the production function, that is the 'frontier' cost function. Førsund and Jansen (1977) used this approach in an efficiency analysis of the Norwegian mechanical pulp industry. The 'cost frontier' approach was also used by Schmidt and Lovell (1979) in a study of efficiency in US steam electric generation industry 1947–65.

Much of what has been written on best practice function is concerned with statistical aspects and the problem of estimating a BP function empirically. Farrell (1958) used the simple method of using the most efficient observations (i.e. those observations with the lowest unit input coefficients) and representatives of the best practice technology. The unit isoquant was constructed as a simple linear combination of those efficient observations. This approach was also used by Seitz (1970; 1971) and Afriat (1972).

Most best practice functions are, however, based on some sort of statistical estimation procedure. The first attempt here was made by Aigner and Chu (1968) which established the frontier simply by minimising the sum distance of observations subject to the restriction that all 'errors' had equal sign. This method was developed further by Afriat (1972) who considered explicitly the statistical assumptions in best practice estimates. This aspect was further developed by Richmond (1974) and Schmidt (1976).

A further development occurred in 1977 with the 'composed error' model of Aigner *et al.* (1977) and Meeusen and van den Broeck (1977). This model assumes a stochastic production function rather than a deterministic one. The error term consists of two parts. One one-sided part which captures the 'efficiency' effect, and one symmetric part which captures the normal statistical errors such as measurement errors, random effects, etc. This 'stochastic frontier' approach was used by Lee and Tyler (1978) and Broeck *et al.* (1980). In the latter part, the authors compared estimations of deterministic and stochastic frontiers.

## 9.14 Empirical Short-run Macro Functions

Empirical illustrations of the Johansen short-run function concept started with Eide (1969) who constructed a macro production function for the Norwegian tanker fleet. This choice of study object was well suited for the model. The capacity of each tanker was fixed uniquely by the speed and the cargo capacity and two variable inputs, labour and fuel, were responsible for the bulk of variable cost.

After the Johansen application, the model was used in the study of the Nordic iron production (Puu and Wibe, 1976) and the Swedish particle board industry (Førsund and Hjalmarsson, 1978). In these, as well as in the original study, the functions were constructed for one year only, thus summarising the (static) nature of the industry. Beginning with the studies of Førsund *et al.* (1980) on the development of the Swedish pulp industry 1920–74, short-run functions were used for the study of technological progress and structural change. By constructing functions for different years in the period (1920, 1929, 1969 and 1974) it was possible to analyse the movements of specific isoquants over time and obtain a good understanding of the advancement of technology. This approach was also used by Wibe (1980) in his long-run study (1850–1975) of the Swedish iron-making industry and by Førsund and Hjalmarsson (1983) in their study of the Swedish cement industry 1955–9. Non-Nordic studies exist (e.g. Hildenbrand's study (1981) of US steam electricity generating plants) but are rare. On the whole, the use of Johansen's model is limited to the Nordic countries.

Short-run macro functions have also been used to compare technology and technological progress. This was done by Wibe (1983a) in an analysis of the Swedish and Finnish pulp industries 1937–54 and by Førsund and Hjalmarsson (1985) in an analysis of the Nordic cement industry.

In all these studies, labour and energy have been the only factors used.

Some developments regarding methodology have also occurred. Johansen (1972) constructed the function simply by ranking the micro units according to unit production cost. This ranking was of course done for a variety of different input prices. The same ranking procedure was used by Puu and Wibe (1976) and Hildenbrand (1981, 1982).

A computer program for a numerical construction of the whole short-run function was developed by Førsund and Hjalmarsson at the University of Oslo. This method was presented in Førsund *et al.* (1980) and later in Førsund and Hjalmarsson (1983). The program also involved methods for calculating the elasticities of scale and substitution, the latter calculated as arc elasticities.

The question of the empirical relevance of the short-run functions were raised in a study of Wibe (1983a). Wibe compared actual factor use with factor use implied by the Johansen assumption in a material consisting of Swedish pulp plants 1929–54. Three different kinds of pulp and three different variable factors (labour, energy and timber) were considered. The results were negative. It was found that there was no correlation between the efficiency of a plant and its degree of capacity utilisation. In case of a general decline in the demand for the industry's product, the most efficient plants cut back their production about as much as the least efficient ones. Thus, a production function based on the inverse economic rule that the most efficient close totally and the least efficient produced fully, would be as empirically correct as the normal short-run function. The results indicate that short-run functions can be used as 'snap-shots' of an industrial structure but they cannot be used as a tool for predicting short-run behaviour in an industry.

## Selected Reading

The statistical problems involved in estimating production functions are analysed in any standard textbook on econometrics, for example R. J. Wonnacott and T. H. Wonnacott, *Econometrics* (1970). The econometric problems involved in estimating production functions are comprehensively discussed in Marshak and Andrews (1944). For the Cobb–Douglas function in particular, see Zellner *et al.* (1966). For the effects of changing the error structure, see Bodkin and Klein (1967) and Mizon (1977). For empirical work on Frontier Production Functions, see for example, Førsund and Hjalmarsson (1974) and Schmidt (1976).

The concept of engineering production function was first used by H. B. Chenery, 'Engineering Production Functions' (1949), *Quarterly Journal of Economics*, LXIII, pp. 507–531. A survey over the area is given in S. Wibe, 'Engineering Production Functions–A Survey' (1984), *Economica*, 51, no. 204, pp. 401–413. A pseudo-data method was first presented in J. M. Griffin, 'The Econometrics of Joint Production: Another Approach' (1977a), *The Review of Economics and Statistics*, 59, pp. 389–97 and criticised in G. S. Maddala and R. Blaine Roberts, 'Alternative Functional Forms and Errors of Pseudo Data Estimation' (1980), *Review of Economics and Statistics*, 62, pp. 323–7.

# Bibliography

Afriat, S. N. (1972) 'Efficiency Estimation of Production Functions', *International Economic Review*, 13, no. 3 (Oct) pp. 568–98.

Aigner, D. J. and S. F. Chu (1968) 'On Estimating the Industry Production Function', *American Economic Review*, 58 (4), pp. 226–39.

Aigner, D. J., C. A. K. Lovell and P. J. Schmidt (1977) 'Formulation and Estimation of Stochastic Frontier Production Function Models', *Journal of Econometrices*, 6, no. 1 (July) 21–37.

Allen, R. G. D. (1938) *Mathematical Analysis for Economists* (London: Macmillan).

Arrow, K. J. (1962) 'The Economic Implications of Learning by Doing', *Review of Economic Studies*, 29, pp. 155–73.

Arrow, K. J., H. B. Chenery, B. Minhas and R. M. Solow (1961) 'Capital-Labor Substitution and Economic Efficiency', *Review of Economics and Statistics*, 43, pp. 225–50.

Belinfante, A. E. (1969) 'Technical Change in the Steam Electric Power Generating Industry', Phd. thesis, University of California.

Berndt, E. R. and L. R. Christensen (1973) 'The Translog Function and the Substitution of Equipment, Structures and Labour in U. S. Manufacturing 1929–1968', *Journal of Econometrics*, 1, pp. 81–114.

Berndt, E. R. and D. O. Wood (1975) 'Technology, Prices and the Derived Demand for Energy', *Review of Economics and Statistics*, 56, pp. 259–68.

Bliss, C. J. (1975) *Capital Theory and the Distribution of Income* (Amsterdam: North-Holland).

Bodkin, R. G. and L. Klein (1967) 'Non-Linear Estimation of Aggregate Production Function', *Review of Economics and Statistics*, Vol. XLIX, pp. 28–44.

Boon, G. K. (1964) *Economic Choice of Human and Physical Factors in Production* (Amsterdam: North-Holland).

Broeck, J., F. R. Førsund, L. Hjalmarsson and W. Meeusen (1980) 'On the Estimation of Deterministic and Stochastic Frontier Production

Functions: A Comparison', *Journal of Econometrics*, 13, 117–38.

Brown, B. W. (1966) 'Comparing Economic and Engineering Estimates of the Production Function', PhD thesis, Johns Hopkins University.

Brown, M. (ed.) (1967) *The Theory and Empirical Analysis of Production* (New York: National Bureau of Economic Research).

Burgess, D. F. (1975) 'Duality Theory and Pitfalls in the Specification of Technologies', *Journal of Econometrics*, 3, pp. 105–21.

Carlsson, S. (1939) *A Study on the Pure Theory of Production* (London: P. S. King & Son Ltd.).

Chamberlain, E. H. (1933) *The Theory of Monopolistic Competition* (Cambridge, Mass.: Harvard University Press).

Chenery, H. B. (1949) 'Engineering Production Functions', *Quarterly Journal of Economics*, 63, pp. 507–31.

Christensen, L. R., D. W. Jorgensen and L. J. Lau (1971) 'Conjugate Duality and the Transcendental Production Function', *Econometrica*, July, pp. 255–6.

Christensen, L. R., D. W. Jorgensen and L. J. Lau (1973) 'Transcendental Logarithmic Production Frontiers', *Review of Economics and Statistics* (Feb.), pp. 28–45.

Clemhout, S. (1968) 'The Class of Homothetic Isoquant Production Functions', *Review of Economic Studies*, 35, pp. 91–104.

Cobb, C. W. and P. H. Douglas (1928) 'A Theory of Production', *American Economic Review*, Papers and Proceedings, 28, pp. 139–65.

Cowing, T. G. (1970) 'Technical Change in Steam-electric Generation: An Engineering Approach', PhD thesis, University of California.

Dano, S. (1966) *Industrial Production Models* (Wien: Springer Verlag).

De Salvo, J. S. (1969) 'A Process Function for Rail Linehaul Operations', *Journal of Transport, Economics and Policy*, 3, pp. 3–27.

Dickinson, H. D. (1954) 'A Note on Dynamic Economics'. *Review of Economic Studies*, 22, pp. 69–79.

Diewert, W. E. (1971) 'An Application of the Shephard Duality Theorem: A Generalized Leontief Production Function', *Journal of Political Economy*, 79 pp. 481–507.

Douglas, P. H. (1934) *The Theory of Wages*, New York: Macmillan.

Douglas, P. H. (1948) 'Are there Laws of Production?', *American Economic Review*, Papers and Proceedings, 28, pp. 139–65.

Douglas, P. H. (1967) 'Comments on the Cobb-Douglas Production Function', in M. Brown (ed.) *The Theory and Empirical Analysis of Production.*

Durand, D. (1937) 'Some Thoughts on Marginal Productivity with Special Reference to Professor Douglas' Analysis', *Journal of Political Economy*, XLV, pp. 740–58.

Eide, E. (1969) 'En metode for konstruksjon av aggregerte korttids produktfunksjoner illustrert med data for den Norske tanfklate', *Memorandum from the Institute of Economics*, University of Oslo, 6 May 1969.

Eide, D. (1979) 'Engineering, Production and Cost Functions for Tankers', Oslo, mimeo, University of Oslo.

Farrell, M. J. (1957) 'The Measurement of Productive Efficiency', *Journal of the Royal Statistical Society*, Series A (General), Part III, 120, pp. 253–90.

Farrell, M. J. and M. Fieldhouse (1962) 'Estimating Efficient Productions Functions under Increasing Returns to Scale', *Journal of the Royal Statistical Society*, Series A. (General), 125, pp. 252–67.

Ferguson, C. E. (1969) *The Neoclassical Theory of Production and Distribution* (Cambridge: Cambridge University Press).

Fisher, F. M. (1971) 'Aggregate Production Function and the Explanation of Wages: A Simulation Experiment', *Review of Economics and Statistics*, 53, pp. 305–25.

Førsund, F. and L. Hjalmarsson (1974) 'On the Measurement of Productive Efficiency', *Swedish Journal of Economics*, 76, pp. 141–54.

Førsund, F. and L. Hjalmarsson (1978) 'Production Functions in Swedish Particle Board Industry', in *Capital in the Production Function* (Paris X. Nanterre: Institut de Recherches en Economie de la Production.

Førsund, F. R. and L. Hjalmarsson (1979a) 'Frontier Production Functions and Technical Progress: A Study of General Milk Processing in Swedish Dairy Plants', *Econometrica*, 47, no. 4 (July) 883–900.

Førsund, F. R., and L. Hjalmarsson, (1979b) 'Generalized Farrell Measures of Efficiency: An Application to Milk Processing in Swedish Dairy Plants', *Economic Journal*, forthcoming.

Førsund, F. R. and L. Hjalmarsson (1983) 'Technical Progress and Structural Change in the Swedish Cement Industry, 1955–1979', *Econometrica*, 51 no. 5, 1449–67.

Førsund, F., L. Hjalmarsson, S. Gaunitz and S. Wibe (1980) 'Technical Progress and Structural Change in the Swedish Pulp Industry 1920–1974', in T. Puu and S. Wibe (eds) *The Economics of Technological Progress* (London: Macmillan).

Førsund, F. R. and E. S. Jansen (1977) 'On Estimating Average and Best Practice Homothetic Production Functions via Cost Functions', *International Economic Review*, 18, no. 2 (June) pp. 463–76.

Førsund, F., C. A. Lovell and P. Schmidt (1980) 'A Survey of Frontier Production Functions and of their Relationship to Efficiency Measurement', *Journal of Econometrics*, 13, pp. 5–25.

Førsund, F. R., S. Gaunitz, L. Hjalmarsson and S. Wibe (1980) 'Technical Progress and Structural Change in the Swedish Pulp Industry 1920–74', in *The Economics of Technological Progress*, T. Puu and S. Wibe (eds) (London: Macmillan).

Frisch, R. (1935a) 'Tekniske og okonomiske produktionslover', Mimeographed Lectures. University of Oslo.

Frisch, R. (1935b) 'The Principle of Substitution. An Example of its Application in the Chocolate Industry', *Nordik Tidskrift for Teknisk Okonomi*, pp. 12–27.

Frisch, R. (1965) *Theory of Production* (Dordrecht: D. Reidel Publishing Company).

Galbraith, J. K. (1952) *American Capitalism* (Boston: Houghton Mifflin).

Griffin, J. M. (1977a) 'The Econometrics of Joint Production: Another Approach', *The Review of Economics and Statistics*, 59, pp. 389–97.

Griffin, J. M. (1977b) 'Long-run Production Modeling with Pseudo Data: Electric Power Generation', *Bell Journal of Economics*, 8, pp. 112–27.

Griffin, J. M. (1978) 'Joint Production Technology: The Case of Petrochemicals', *Econometrica*, 46 pp. 379–96.

Griffin, J. M. (1979) 'Statistical Cost Analysis Revisited', *Quarterly Journal of Economics*, 93 pp. 107–130.

Griffin, J. M. (1980) 'Alternative Functional Forms and Errors of Pseudo Data Estimation: A Reply', *Review of Economics and Statistics*, 62 pp. 327–8.

Grosse, A. P. (1953) 'The Technological Structure of the Cotton Textile Industry', in W. Leontief (ed.), *Studies in the Structure of the American Economy* (New York: Oxford University Press).

Harcourt, G. C. (1972) *Some Cambridge Controversies in the Theory of Capital* (Cambridge: Cambridge University Press).

Heady, E. O. and Dillon, J. L. (1961) *Agricultural Production Functions* (Ann Arbor: Iowa State University Press).

Hicks, J. R. (1932) *The Theory of Wages* (London: Macmillan).

Hildebrand, H. (1981). 'Short-Run Production Functions based on Micro Data', *Econometrica*, 49, No. 4, pp. 1095–1124.

Hildenbrand, K. (1982) 'Numerical Computation of Short-run Production Functions', in *Quantitative Studies on Production and Prices*, W. Eichhorn, R. Henn, K. Neumann, and R. W. Shephard (eds). Vienna: (Physica-Verlag).

Houthakker, H. (1955–6) 'The Pareto Distribution and the Cobb–Douglas Production Function in Activity Analysis', *Review of Economics and Statistics*, 22, pp. 27–31.

Hurther, A. D. Jnr. (1962) 'A Production Function for an Industrial Process: Petroleum Refining', PhD thesis, Northwestern University.

Johansen, L. (1959) 'Substitution Versus Fixed Production Coefficients in the Theory of Economic Growth–A Synthesis', *Review of Economics and Statistics*, 22, pp. 157–76.

Johansen, L. (1972) *Production Functions* (Amsterdam: North-Holland).

Johnson, W. E. (1913) 'The Pure Theory of Utility Curves', *Economic Journal*, 22, pp. 483–513.

Kennedy, C. and A. P. Thirlwall (1972) 'Technical Progress: A Survey'. *Economic Journal*, Vol. 82, pp. 11–72.

Kmenta, J. (1967) 'On the Estimation of the C. E. S. Production Function', *International Economic Review*, pp. 180–89.

Kopp, R. J., and V. Kerry Smith (1980a) 'Measuring Factor Substitution with Neoclassical Models: An Experimental Evaluation', *Bell Journal of Economics*, 11, 631–55.

Kopp, R. J. and V. Kerry Smith (1980b) 'Input Substitution, Aggregation and Engineering Descriptions of Production Activities', *Economic Letters*, 5, 289–96.

Kopp, R. J. and V. Kerry Smith (1983) 'Neoclassical Modeling on Non-Neutral Technological Change: An Experimental Appraisal', *Scandinavian Journal of Economics*, 85, 127–46.

Kopp, R. J. and V. Kerry Smith (1985) 'The Measurement of Non-Neutral Technological Change', *International Economic Review*, 26, forthcoming.

Kregel, J. (1976) *Theory of Capital* (London: Macmillan).

Kurtz, M. and A. S. Manne, (1963) 'Engineering Estimates of Capital-Labor Substitution in Metal Machining', *American Economic Review*, 53, pp. 662–81.

Lamyai, T. (1978) 'Microanalytical Investigation of Mechanical Engineering Production Processes', PhD thesis, Northwestern University.

Lee, L. F., and W. G. Tyler (1978) 'The Stochastic Frontier Production Function and Average Efficiency: An Empirical Analysis', *Journal of Econometrics*, 7, No. 3, June, 385–90.

Leontief, W. (ed.) (1953) *Studies in the Structure of the American Economy* (New York: Oxford University Press).

Maddala, G. S. and R. B. Roberts (1980) 'Alternative Functional Forms and Errors of Pseudo Data Estimation', *Review of Economics and Statistics*, 62, pp. 323–7.

Malcomson, J. M. and M. J. Prior (1972) 'The Estimation of a Vintage Model of Production for U. K. Manufacturing', *Review of Economic Studies*, 46.

Mansfield, E. (1969) *The Economics of Technological Change* (London: Longmans).

Marsden, J., Piysy, D. and Whiston, A. (1974) 'Engineering Foundations of Production Functions', *Journal of Economic Theory* vol. 9. pp. 124–40.

Marshak, J. and W. H. Andrews (1944) 'Random Simultaneous Equations and the Theory of Production', *Econometrica*, 12, pp. 143–205.

Meeusen, W. and J. van den Broeck (1977) 'Efficiency Estimation from Cobb-Douglas Production Functions with Composed Error', *International Economic Review*, 18, no. 2 (June) pp. 435–44.

Mizon, G. E. (1977) 'Inferential Procedures in Nonlinear Models: An Application in a U. K. Industrial Cross Section Study of Factor Substitution and Returns to Scale', *Econometrica*, 45, pp. 1221–42.

Nerlove, M. (1967) 'Recent Empirical Studies of the C. E. S. and Related Production Functions', in M. Brown (ed.) *The Theory and Empirical Analysis of Production* (New York: NBER).

Pearl, D. I. and J. L. Enos, (1975) 'Engineering Production Functions and Technological Progress', *Journal of Industrial Economics*, 24, pp. 55–72.

Puu, R. (1966). 'Les Effets de Substitution et D'Expansion Dans la Theorie de la Production', *Revue D'Economie Politique*, 76, pp. 57–91.

Puu, T. (1968) 'Complementarity, Substitutivity and Regressivity in the Theory of Production', *Recherches Recentes sur la Fonction de Production* (v. a.) Facultes Universitaires N. -D. de la Paix, Namur.

Puu, T. and S. Wibe (1976) 'Produktionsfunktioner for den nordiska masugs-producktionen enligt Leif Johansens modell. (Production Functions for the Nordic Blast Furnace Production According to Leif Johansen's Model). *Umea Economic Studies* No. 24, Umea University, Sweden.

Ricardo, D. (1946) 'On the Principles of Political Economy and Taxation', in McCulloch (ed.), *The Works of David Ricardo* (London).

Richmond, J. (1974) 'Estimating the Efficiency of Production', *International Economic Review*, 15, no. 2 (June) pp. 515–21.

Robinson, J. (1933) *The Economics of Imperfect Competition* (London: Macmillan).

Robinson, J. (1960) *Exercises in Economic Analysis*. (London: Macmillan).
Salter, W. E. G. (1960) *Productivity and Technical Change* (Cambridge University Press).
Samuelson, P. (1947) *Foundations of Economic Analysis* (Cambridge University Press).
Schmidt, P. (1976) 'On the Statistical Estimation of Parametric Frontier Production Functions', *Review of Economics and Statistics*, 58, no. 2 (May). pp. 238–9.
Schmidt, P. and C. A. K. Lovell (1979) 'Estimating Technical and Allocative Inefficiency Relative to Stochastic Production and Cost Frontiers', *Journal of Econometrics*, 9, no. 3 (Feb. pp. 343–66.
Schneider, E. (1934) *Theorie de Production* (Wien: Julius Springer).
Schott, K. (1976) 'Investment in Private Industrial Research and Development in Britain', *Journal of Industrial Economics*, 25, pp. 81–99.
Schumpeter, J. (1939) *Business Cycles* (New York: McGraw-Hill).
Schumpeter, J. (1947) *Capitalism, Socialism and Democracy* (New York: Harper and Row).
Schumpeter, J. (1954) *History of Economic Analysis* (New York: Oxford University Press).
Seip, D. (1974) 'A Geometrical Approach to Aggregation from Micro to Macro in Putty-Clay Aggregated Production Functions', Memorandum from the Institute of Economics, University of Oslo.
Seitz, W. D. (1970) 'The Measurement of Efficiency Relative to a Frontier Production Function', *American Journal of Agricultural Economics*, 52, no. 4 (Nov.), pp. 505–511.
Seitz, W. D. (1971) 'Productive Efficiency in the Steam-electric Generating Industry', *Journal of Political Economy*, 79, no. 4 (July/Aug.) pp. 878–86.
Shephard, R. W. (1953) *Cost and Production Functions* (Princeton: Princeton University Press).
Smith, V. L. (1961) *Investment and Production* (Cambridge: Harvard University Press).
Solow, R. M. (1974) 'Laws of Production and Laws of Algebra: A Humbug Production Function: A Comment', *Review of Economics and Statistics*, p. 121.
Sraffa, P. (1972) Production of Commodities By Means of Commodities (Cambridge University Press).
Stubbs, P. C. and J. S. Metcalfe (1980) Bibliography, in T. Puu and S. Wibe (eds), *The Economics of Technological Progress* (London: Macmillan).
Timmer, C. P. (1971) 'Using a Probabilistic Frontier Production Function to Measure Technical Efficiency', *Journal of Political Economy*, 79, no. 4 (July/Aug.), pp. 776–94.
Vazquez, A. (1971) 'Homogeneous Production Functions with Constant or Variable Elasticity of Substitution', *Zeitschrift fur die Gesamte Staatswissenschaft*, pp. 7–26.
Von Shaik, A. (1974) 'Laws of Production and Laws of Algebra: A Humbug Production Function', *Review of Economics and Statistics*, pp. 115–20.
Von Thünen, J. H. (1826) *Der Isolierte Staat in Bezeiehung auf Landwirtschaft und Nationalokonomie*. Jena.

Wibe, S. (1980) 'Teknik och Aggregering i Produktionsteorin (Technology and Aggregation in Production Theory). Phd. thesis.

Wibe, S. (1983a) 'The Empirical Relevance of Short Run Efficiency', *Umea Economic Studies No* 126, Umea University, Sweden.

Wibe, S. (1983b) 'An International Comparison of Technology and Technological Development – A Case Study', *Umea Economic Studies*, No. 131, Umea University, Sweden.

Wibe, S. (1984) 'Engineering Production Functions: A Survey', *Economica*, 51 No. 204 (Nov.), pp. 401–413.

Wonnacott, R. J. and T. H. Wonnacott (1970) *Econometrics* (New York: Wiley).

Zellner, A., J. Kmenta and J. Dreze (1966) 'The Specification and Estimation of Cobb-Douglas Production Models', *Econometrica*, vol. 34, pp. 784–95.

Zellner, A. and N. S. Revankar (1969) 'Generalized Production Functions', *Review of Economic Studies*, vol. 36, pp. 241–50.

# Index